WW II

International Aircraft

Recognition

Manual

AVIATION
PUBLICATIONS

217 E. WASHINGTON ST.
P. O. BOX 357
APPLETON
WISCONSIN
54912
U.S.A.

ISBN No. 0-87994-017-4

THE FIRST REQUIREMENT in warfare is the ability to distinguish friend from foe. Nowhere is this more difficult than in the air. Owing to the great speeds and heights attained by modern aircraft, recognition is frequently dependent on a momentary glimpse. In the same way instant and accurate recognition of surface craft, mechanized ground equipment, etc., is fraught with great difficulties owing to varying conditions of visibility, distance, and variety of types.

Before the outbreak of this war few realized the grave problems of recognition that the increasing dominance of air power would present. The existence of these problems was soon apparent when, after two months, the casualties of the British Advanced Air Striking Force in France amounted to:—Shot down by the Germans, eight: Shot down by the French, nine. In those days the only question asked was, "Is it in range?" Since then mistakes in recognition, on the sea, on land, and in the air have been too numerous to mention. Usually these mistakes are attended by the most serious consequences.

It is now fully realized that the only way to prevent these occurrences is by demanding the highest general level of proficiency in recognition throughout the services. This can only be attained by concentrated study. It is not suggested that practice will make one absolutely perfect, but it will certainly go most of the way toward reducing the chances of a man being a danger not only to himself, but to his comrades-in-arms.

The Navy's problem at sea, whether on warship or merchant ship, is to know as soon as possible whether any aircraft or ship within sight is friendly or hostile, what type it is, and how it is likely to attack, and from that to estimate the best method of defence.

The Army's problems are also varied. Antiaircraft gunners should be able to recognize any airplane within range, or likely to come within range, whether flying directly toward the battery or not. Columns on the move may have to contend with the low-flying attack-bomber or the dive-bomber. Instant recognition saves lives and leads to the destruction of the enemy.

The Air Forces, both of the Army and the Navy, have even more problems to solve because the views from which crews may see the enemy are not confined to those from underneath. The fighter pilot may hope to dive on the enemy from above and behind, but to him the underneath view is important too. The tail gunner needs the head-on view. All must know their aircraft well. In a completely different category are the photographic interpreters who have to recognize the top-plan views of aircraft dispersed on airdromes or in ports. In the past, too little attention has been paid to this important silhouette. Likewise, the accurate recognition of mechanized ground equipment is of extreme importance.

The Ground Observer Corps has concentrated much attention on recognition. Again any aircraft within view, friendly or hostile, should be recognized quickly—even through a momentary gap in the clouds.

The first thing to be appreciated is that recognition does not begin and end with appearance. Certainly it is essential to distinquish between the appearance of friend and foe; *but this is seldom sufficient*. It is also essential to recognize the exact type. In the

U.S.A. **U.K.**

FRIEND

PV VENTURA MB	**P-47** THUNDERBOLT F	**A-30** BALTIMORE LB	**P-51** MUSTANG F	**PBY** CATALINA, PB
A-35 (A-31) VENGEANCE DB	**A-20** HAVOC BOSTON LB-F	**SNJ** TEXAN AT	**B-24** LIBERATOR HB-TR	**SO3C** SEAGULL R
C-60 LODESTAR TR	**F4U** CORSAIR F	**B-25** MITCHELL MB	**TBF** AVENGER TB	**PBM** MARINER PB-TR
SB2C HELLDIVER DB	**P-38** LIGHTNING F	**F6F** HELLCAT F	**B-17** FLYING FORTRESS HB	**P-40** WARHAWK F
A-29 HUDSON LB	**SBD** DAUNTLESS DB	**B-26** MARAUDER MB	**F4F** WILDCAT F	**C-47** SKYTRAIN C-53 SKYTROOPER TR. GLIDER TUG

GB-1 TRAVELER UTILITY	**BEAUFIGHTER** F	**HALIFAX** HB	**SKUA** DB-F
C-54 SKYMASTER TR	**ALBACORE** TB	**HURRICANE** LB-F	**SUNDERLAND** PB
P-39 AIRACOBRA —	**BEAUFORT** LB	**LANCASTER** HB	**SPITFIRE** F
PB2Y CORONADO PB	**MOSQUITO** LB-F	**TYPHOON** F	**STIRLING** HB.
OS2U KINGFISHER R	**BARRACUDA** R	**WELLINGTON** MB	**BERMUDA** DB

INTRODUCTION

case of aircraft, this recognition gives knowledge of the wing span, approximate speed, probable armament, and if hostile, a reasonable deduction as to future actions. The situation is similar to that of surface-craft, where recognition has a tactical value and gives an idea of what the enemy can do and how he may be dealt with, once recognized.

What enables a person accurately and speedily to recognize tanks, ships, planes, etc.? The process is no different from that of recognizing an automobile, a horse, a bird, or a friend. Let one ask himself the question, "When I see a friend walking down the street, do I look at every feature of him and having gone through a process of analysis, decide that it is Bill?" Obviously not. Recognition is instinctive. One knows immediately that it is "Bill" because one is *familiar* with his whole appearance and general characteristics, such as the way he stands or walks. It is not difficult to translate these characteristics into terms of airplanes, ships, etc. The combination of all these characteristics into the over-all effect of an object is known scientifically as the "total form" of that object. Now one can ask one more question. "Why did you get to know the "total form" of a friend or automobile, or horse?" The answer is, because you were interested in him or it. Therefore, the requirement for efficient recognition is familiarity based on a general knowledge of air or surface craft, or tanks, or other military equipment, a knowledge which will only be gained by an aroused interest and enthusiasm for them. If this is borne in mind, there will finally be an end to those famous last words, "I *think* they're ours."

NOTE:

"RECOGNITION" means VISUAL recognition.

"IDENTIFICATION" means identification OTHER THAN VISUAL.

PICTORIAL MANUAL

The present manual is primarily designed for self-instruction and general use but will also serve as a text in recognition courses. It includes four types of material: black and white silhouettes; wash drawings; photographs; and editorial matter.

Silhouettes are the foundation stone on which all recognition training is based. They may seem dull and uninspiring but the fact remains that the "three-view" silhouette, giving the head-on, plan, and side-view shows every salient recognition feature of a ship or plane just as an architect's drawing of plan, section, and elevations gives the essentials of a building. They are basic diagrams and their value is evident from the accompanying example which shows how great is the contrast between the halves of two different airplanes and indicates in print the facts which an experienced observer can read directly from a silhouette. The wash drawings pick up where the silhouette diagrams leave off. By adding form and detail, they advance toward reality while still conveying accurate facts like engineering drawings. Both types of drawing should be studied for their over-all effect and not just for details. Photographs give the final step toward a realistic impression and show the aircraft, etc., from various angles. The editorial matter is intended to drive home the plane or ship by lending it interest and appeal; also such data are included as can be released.

The material in this manual has been assembled and edited jointly by Army and Navy aviation training divisions. Much valuable assistance has been contributed by the British, particularly in supplying silhouettes. The bulk of the material came from intelli-

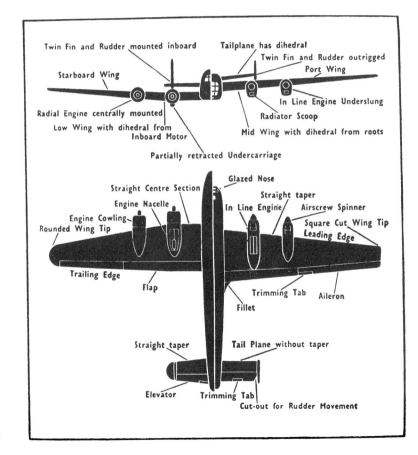

gence and photographic sources in both Army and Navy. The data and dimensions are the most exact available. The Army and Navy can release only approximate performance figures for their own planes and ships but the dimensions given have been obtained from their respective design sections. For foreign models, the best available figures are given and, where reliable sources of information differ on dimensions, the more probable figure is given and the less probable one follows it in parenthesis. It is suggested that when figures are definitely confirmed, the necessary corrections be made by the individual holding this book. The manual will be constantly enlarged and amended.

MOTION PICTURES

An ideal form of training would naturally be to see actual aircraft, ships, etc., as often as required until one was entirely familiar with them in all positions and under every condition of visibility. This is clearly impracticable; therefore the training medium which reproduces this ideal with the greatest realism is the moving picture. There are, at present, three types of training film available. The first is introductory and is intended for presentation in the primary stages of training. Its object is to serve as a glossary of terms explaining to the beginner the meaning of such words and phrases as "dihedral", "taper", "underslung", etc. The second kind of film is that dealing with the recognition of individual types of aircraft, ships, etc. This class of film is planned on the principle that it is of basic importance to have detailed knowledge. Flying or action shots are combined with close-up stills, diagrams, and animated drawings, all joining with the commentary to give the visual directive to the human eye which is so essential. This series may be used effectively, provided detailed analysis is not accepted as a final solution to the problem. An airplane, for example, cannot be learned just by memorizing its wings, engines, fuselage, and tail, separately and without regard to the "total form" effect they join to produce; for in recognition the whole is more than the sum of its parts. The third class of film is well represented by the "Quizcraft" Series. This class comprises actual flying shots of various aircraft and is designed for use at a more advanced stage of training. It is not suggested that these films present a serious recognition problem to a man with any degree of training. The primary object is to give the student the opportunity to see aircraft in conditions as nearly as possible approaching reality. Emphasis, therefore, is placed upon distant shots under all conditions of visibility. The "test" element is secondary and only introduced to maintain interest. Training films and film strips are listed in FM 21-7 and in the Catalog of U. S. Navy Training films.

FILM SLIDES AND FILM STRIPS

Film slides and film strips are another means of presenting silhouettes, wash-drawings, and still photographs. By reducing progressively the time of exposing them, it is possible to develop speed in recognition. Time intervals as short as one-fifth second can be obtained with an improvised shutter consisting of a piece of cardboard with a hole in it which is allowed to drop across the projector lens.

FOE

Reich				Japan			Italy	
F. W. 190 — F	Do 26 — PB	ME 210 — LB-F	Do 217 — HB	NELL — MB	SONIA — LB R	IDA — LB	Re-2001 — F	SM-79 — MB-TR
Ju 290 — TR-HB	ARADO 196 — R	Ju 52 — TR GLIDER TUG	HE 115 — TB-R	CLAUDE — F	BETTY — MB	MARY — LB	CANT. Z-1007 — MB	MC-202 — F
HE 113 — F	F. W. 200 — HB-TR	F. W. 189 — R	GOTHA 242 — GLIDER	MAVIS — PB	PETE — R	IONE — TB	FIAT G-50 — F	BR-20 — MB-TR
Ju 90 — TR-HB	Ju 87 STUKA — DB	HA 138 — PB	HE 111 — MB	NATE — F	TOPSY — TR	DAVE — R	ZEKE ZERO — F	RUFE — ZERO FLOAT
ME 109 — F	HE 177 — HB	ME 110 — LB-F	Ju 88 — MB-F	SALLY — MB	VAL — DB	KATE — TB	HAP — SQUARE TIP ZERO	

EACH LARGE SQUARE 100 FT. x 100 FT.

FLASH METER TRAINING

This is a development in the method of projecting film slides perfected for use by the U. S. Navy. It has also been adopted, with certain modifications, by the U. S. Army Air Forces. Equipment is used which consists of a slide projector with a flash meter (like a camera shutter). The slides are flashed on the screen at progressively faster speeds up to 1/100th second. At such speeds, the student is forced to recognize an object from its "total form" because there is no time for the eye to scan its parts. The importance of this approach has already been mentioned. This develops a "skill of seeing" and holds the student's attention like a game of skill. For fullest application, a properly trained instructor is necessary.

MODELS AND POSTERS

Sets of scale models of aircraft and surface craft are obtainable in accordance with existing regulations and policies. These models are highly accurate and carefully constructed to scale. Suspending airplane models in various flying attitudes or setting out ship models in formation is all very well as far as it goes, but even more important is it that they should be available to students for examination. They may satisfy themselves, the models being accurate, that certain features do exist which may well have been missed when seeing representations of the aircraft or ship on former occasions. The scale model is eminently suitable as it can be made to adopt any position, whereas the views presented by slides, photographs, and silhouettes are necessarily limited.

Posters are valuable for teaching classes if no projector is available. Posted conspicuously, they constantly refresh the memory.

TEACHING RECOGNITION

The above training aids can best be utilized for teaching recognition if training progresses as follows. FIRST, the student is taught the important items of nomenclature using the glossary in this manual, supplemented by the introductory training films and film strips. SECOND, individual planes, ships, etc., are presented, with emphasis on their silhouette, engineering form, photographic appearance, and interest appeal. In addition to this manual, large posters of silhouettes or wash-drawings may be used. Silhouettes, wash-drawings, or photographs can also be projected on screens using delineoscopes or film slides or strips. THIRD, the student's attention must thereafter be directed to recognizing the "total form" of the object. For this purpose, motion pictures (on individual airplanes, ships, etc.) and models can be utilized to good advantage. Film slides and film strips projected for progressively decreasing periods of time are the best means of presenting "total form" and *should be utilized to the maximum extent to which these aids are available*. FINALLY, the aircraft, etc., are observed under the most realistic conditions possible, as in the "Quizcraft" series of motion pictures. Where necessary the ingenious recognition instructor should improvise his own aids and equipment. Cases are reported where an opaque projector (i. e. reflectoscope) was concocted from a box, bulbs, old lenses, cardboard tube, etc. In this, as in any other enterprise of war, improvisation will often be the rule and not the exception.

In conclusion, PRACTICAL RESULTS ARE THE FINAL TEST AND A STUDENT MUST TRY HIS SKILL ON EVERY ACTUAL SHIP OR PLANE HE SEES AND ON EVERY PICTURE OF ONE IN A MAGAZINE OR NEWSPAPER.

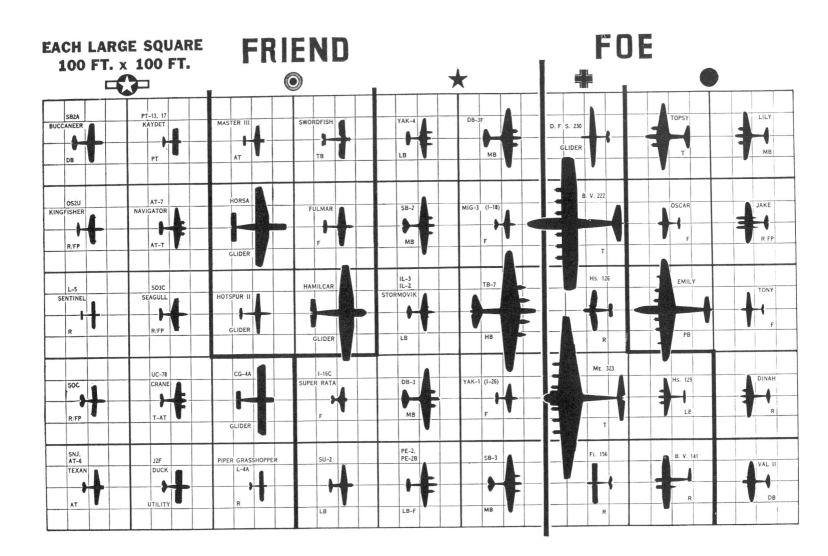

EACH LARGE SQUARE
100 FT. x 100 FT.

FRIEND

FOE

SB2A BUCCANEER — DB	PT–13, 17 KAYDET — PT	MASTER III — AT	SWORDFISH — TB	YAK–4 — LB	DB–3F — MB	D. F. S. 230 GLIDER	TOPSY — T	LILY — MB
OS2U KINGFISHER — R/FP	AT–7 NAVIGATOR — AT–T	HORSA — GLIDER	FULMAR — F	SB–2 — MB	MIG–3 (I–18) — F	B. V. 222 — T	OSCAR — F	JAKE — R FP
L–5 SENTINEL — R	SO3C SEAGULL — R/FP	HOTSPUR II — GLIDER	HAMILCAR — GLIDER	IL–3 IL–2 STORMOVIK — LB	TB–7 — HB	Hs. 126 — R	EMILY — PB	TONY — F
SOC — R/FP	UC–78 CRANE — T–AT	CG–4A — GLIDER	I–16C SUPER RATA — F	DB–3 — MB	YAK–1 (I–26) — F	ME. 323 — T	Hs. 129 — LE	DINAH — R
SNJ, AT–6 TEXAN — AT	J2F DUCK — UTILITY	PIPER GRASSHOPPER L–4A — R	SU–2 — LB	PE–2, PE–2B — LB–F	SB–3 — MB	FI. 156 — R	B. V. 141 — R	VAL II — DB

The purpose of inserting a glossary into this manual is to enable all who use it to describe an airplane by the same terms. By no means does it pretend to be an encyclopedia of aeronautical and aerodynamical science but rather a reference page to define those visible features of any airplane by which it is most readily recognized.

AILERON—Hinged, movable portion of wing, usually at trailing edge, whose primary function is to induce a rolling motion on the airplane.

AIRFOIL—Any surface, such as an airplane wing, aileron, or rudder designed to obtain reaction from the air through which it moves.

AIR SCOOP—A scoop or hood designed to catch the air and maintain the air pressure in internal-combustion engines, ventilators, etc.

AMPHIBIAN—An airplane designed to rise from and alight on either land or water.

ANGLE OF INCIDENCE—The acute angle between the plane of the wing chord and the horizontal axis of the airplane. The angle is positive when the leading edge is higher than the trailing edge.

ARRESTER HOOK—The device lowered by a carrier based airplane to facilitate limited-space landings.

ARRESTING GEAR—The mechanism on an airplane and on the landing area used in limited-space landings.

AUTOGIRO—A type of rotor plane whose support in the air is normally derived from airfoils aerodynamically rotated about an approximately vertical axis, and whose forward speed is supplied by engine and propeller.

BALANCED SURFACE—A control surface that extends on both sides of the hinge line, or that has auxiliary extensions to effect a balance on the hinge line. Used frequently on rudders, ailerons, and elevators.

"BELLY"—Colloquial term for ventral portion of fuselage.

BIPLANE—An airplane with two wings placed one over the other.

"BLISTER"—A colloquial term for a streamlined transparent housing protruding from the fuselage, containing movable armament.

BRACING—Struts, guys, or other stiffeners used to brace any part of the structure of an airplane, externally or internally.

CABANE—An arrangement of struts.

CABIN—Compartment for one or more persons built entirely within the profile of the fuselage.

CAMBER—The curvature of an airfoil from the mean line of its chord section.

CANOPY—A hood, covering, or enclosure.

CENTER SECTION—The central panel of a wing.

CHORD—The straight line joining the leading and trailing edges of an airfoil, also called "chord length."

COCKPIT—An open space in an airplane to accommodate the pilot and/or other persons.

COWLING—A removable covering, as over a cockpit, or around part—or all—of an engine.

DIHEDRAL ANGLE—The acute angle between the longitudinal center line of the wing and an imaginary horizontal line. When a plane has positive dihedral the wings slope "up."

DIVE BRAKE—A flap or slat which, when opened, reduces the speed of the airplane in a dive.

DORSAL—Pertaining to the back or top portion of the fuselage.

EDGE-LEADING—The entering or forward portion of an airfoil or propeller blade.

TRAILING—The after or rearmost portion of an airfoil or propeller blade.

ELEVATOR—A movable auxiliary airfoil usually hinged to the stabilizer. Its function is to induce a pitching motion on the airplane.

ENGINE—The motive power of an aircraft. "Radial" and "in-line" refer to the placement of cylinders about the propeller shaft. The former type is usually air-cooled; the latter generally liquid-cooled.

FIN—A fixed or adjustable airfoil to afford directional stability, such as a tail fin or skid fin, etc.

FLAP—A hinged or pivoted airfoil forming the rear

GLOSSARY

portion of an airfoil, used to vary the effective camber.

FLOAT—A completely enclosed watertight structure attached to an aircraft to give it buoyancy and stability when in contact with water.

FLOAT, inboard stabilizing— A stabilizing float placed relatively close to the main float or hull.

FLOAT, outboard (or wing-tip) stabilizing— A stabilizing float placed relatively far out from the main float or hull, usually at or very near the tip of the wing.

FLOAT, stabilizing (or side)—A float used in addition to a single float or hull and intended to provide lateral stability while the seaplane or flying boat is at rest on the water.

FLYING BOAT—A form of seaplane whose main body or hull provides flotation.

FUSELAGE—The body, of approximately streamline form, to which the wings and tail unit of an airplane are attached.

GAP—The distance separating two adjacent wings of a multiplane.

"GILL RING"—The adjustable after portion of the cowling of a radial engine used to effect efficient air cooling.

GLIDER—An aircraft heavier than air, similar to an airplane but without a power plant.

PRIMARY-TYPE GLIDER—A ruggedly built glider designed for use in elementary training of student glider pilots.

SECONDARY-TYPE GLIDER—A glider designed to have better aerodynamic performance

than the primary type. but rugged enough for the use of pilots with limited training.

PERFORMANCE-TYPE GLIDER—A glider having a high degree of aerodynamic refinement and low minimum sinking speed.

"GREENHOUSE"—Colloquial term for the transparent canopy or hood over the cockpit.

HEIGHT—The vertical measurement of an airplane at rest; taken from the lowest point of contact to the topmost part of the airplane including the rotation arc of the propeller.

HELICOPTER—A type of rotor plane whose support in the air is normally derived from airfoils mechanically rotated about an approximately vertical axis.

HINGE LINE—The joint between a fixed and a movable surface, such as wing and aileron, stabilizer and elevator, fin and rudder.

HOOD—A covering, canopy, or cowling, usually applied to the fuselage.

HOUSING—A covering over a space used to enclose a movable part such as a retractable wheel gear.

HUB—The center portion of a propeller or wheel about which rotation occurs.

HULL, SEAPLANE—That portion of a flying boat which furnishes buoyancy when in contact with the surface of the water. It contains accommodations for the crew and passengers, usually combining the functions of both float and fuselage.

LANDING GEAR—The gear on the underside of the fuselage which supports an aircraft in take-off or landing.

LANDPLANE—An airplane which rises from and alights on land.

LENGTH (OVER-ALL)—The extreme forward-aft measurement of an airplane.

LOOP—Radio antenna formed of coils of wire.

MAST, RADIO—A fixed spar attached to an aircraft used for supporting a radio antenna.

MONOCOQUE—Term applied to fuselage construction which relies on the strength of the skin or shell for its structural stiffness. The shell is reinforced vertically by structural bulkheads.

MONOPLANE—An aircraft with a single plane or wing. There are four general types:

LOW-WING—A monoplane whose wing is located at—or near—the bottom of the fuselage.

MID-WING—A monoplane whose wing is located at approximately the midpoint between top and bottom of fuselage.

HIGH-WING—A monoplane whose wing is located at the top of the fuselage.

PARASOL-WING—A monoplane whose wing is above the top of the fuselage and is supported by a cabane or other connection.

MULTIPLANE—An airplane having two or more wings, superimposed.

NACELLE—An enclosed shelter for personnel or for a power plant. A nacelle is usually shorter than a fuselage, and does not carry the tail unit.

NOSE—The foremost part of the fuselage.

OVERHANG—(1) One half the difference in span of any two wings of an airplane. (2) The distance from the outer strut attachment to the wing tip.

PANEL (AIRPLANE)—A portion of an airplane wing constructed separately from the rest of the wing to which it is attached.

"PANTS"—Colloquial term for the housing of non-retractable landing gear struts.

PROFILE THICKNESS—The maximum distance between the upper and lower contours of an airfoil, measured perpendicularly to the mean line of the profile.

PROPELLER—Any device for propelling a craft through a fluid, such as water or air; especially a device having blades which, when mounted on a power-driven shaft, produce a thrust by their action on the fluid.

ADJUSTABLE PROPELLER—A propeller whose blades are so attached to the hub that the pitch may be changed while the propeller is at rest.

AUTOMATIC PROPELLER—A propeller whose blades are attached to a mechanism that automatically sets them at their optimum pitch for various flight conditions.

CONTROLLABLE PROPELLER—A propeller whose blades are so mounted that the pitch may be changed while the propeller is rotating.

GEARED PROPELLER—A propeller driven through gearing, generally at some speed other than the engine speed.

PUSHER PROPELLER—A propeller mounted on the rear end of the engine or propeller shaft.

TRACTOR PROPELLER—A propeller mounted on the forward end of the engine or propeller shaft.

RETRACTABLE LANDING GEAR—A type of landing gear which may be withdrawn into the body, nacelle, or wings of an airplane during flight in order to reduce parasitic drag.

RIB—A chord-wise structural member of the wing.

RING COWLING—A ring-shaped cowling placed around a radial air-cooled engine to reduce its drag and improve cooling.

ROOT—The "base" of the wing where it is attached to the fuselage.

ROTOR—The complete rotating portion of a rotary wing system.

ROTOR PLANE—A form of aircraft whose support in the air is chiefly derived from the vertical component of the force produced by rotating airfoils.

RUDDER—A hinged, auxiliary vertical airfoil whose function is to induce yaw or side-to-side motion on an aircraft.

SAILPLANE—A performance-type glider.

SEAPLANE—An airplane designed to rise from and alight on the water.

SESQUIPLANE—A form of biplane in which the area of one wing is less than half the area of the other.

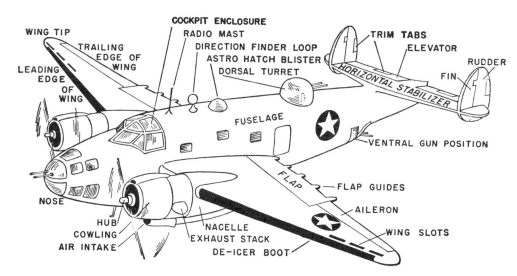

WING TIP · TRAILING EDGE OF WING · LEADING EDGE OF WING · NOSE · HUB · COWLING · AIR INTAKE · COCKPIT ENCLOSURE · RADIO MAST · DIRECTION FINDER LOOP · ASTRO HATCH BLISTER · DORSAL TURRET · FUSELAGE · FLAP · NACELLE · EXHAUST STACK · DE-ICER BOOT · TRIM TABS · ELEVATOR · RUDDER · HORIZONTAL STABILIZER · FIN · VENTRAL GUN POSITION · FLAP GUIDES · AILERON · WING SLOTS

GLOSSARY

SHAFT—The part connected to the power plant which drives the propeller or rotor (of a helicopter).

SKID FIN—A fore and aft vertical surface, usually attached to the top of the wing to increase lateral stability.

SLAT—A movable auxiliary airfoil, attached to the leading edge of a wing, which when closed falls within the original contour of the main wing and which when opened forms a slot.

SLOT—The space between the "slat" and wing designed to improve the flow conditions of an airfoil.

SLOTTED AILERON—An aileron having an air passage between the nose of the aileron and the wing.

SPAN—The maximum distance from tip to tip of an airfoil.

"SPAT"—An aerodynamically designed housing to cover a nonretractable wheel.

SPINNER—A fairing of approximately conical or paraboloidal shape, which is fitted coaxially with the propeller hub and revolves with the propeller.

SPOILER—A small plate arranged to project above the upper surface of a wing to disturb the smooth air flow, with consequent loss of lift and increase of drag.

SPONSON—A protuberance from a seaplane hull designed to increase the beam or give lateral stability at rest.

SPRAY STRIP—A strip projecting from the hull of a seaplane to change the manner in which the spray is thrown.

STABILIZER—Any airfoil whose primary function is to increase the stability of an aircraft. It usually refers to the fixed horizontal tail surface of an airplane, as distinguished from the fixed vertical surface.

STABILIZER, STUB-WING—A projection from the side of the central hull of a flying boat intended to increase the buoyancy and stability of a flying boat while the boat is at rest and to increase the hydrodynamic lift during the take-off. It is an integral part of the hull, and usually takes the form of a stumpy airfoil or a stub wing.

STEP—A break in the form of the bottom of a float or hull.

STRUT—A member of a truss frame.

OLEO STRUT—A shock absorbing telescoping strut in which an oleo gear is used.

SWEEPBACK—Term applied to a wing whose leading and trailing edges are further aft at the tips than at the center.

TAB—An auxiliary airfoil attached to a control surface for the purpose of reducing the control force or trimming the aircraft.

TAIL—The after part of an airplane consisting of stabilizers, elevators, fin, and rudder.

TAIL BOOM—A spar or outrigger connecting the tail surfaces and the main supporting surfaces.

TAIL SKID—A skid for supporting the tail of an airplane on the ground.

TAIL WHEEL—A wheel for supporting the tail of an airplane on the ground.

TAPER—A gradual diminishing of the chord length or chord thickness of an airfoil.

TIP—The outermost part of an airfoil or propeller.

TURRET—A transparent movable enclosure housing armament. It may be free or power-driven. It may also be retractable.

UNDERCARRIAGE—See landing gear.

VENTRAL—The lowermost part of a fuselage.

WING—Main supporting surface or airfoil of an airplane. It can have many plan shapes, the most usual of which are:

(a) STRAIGHT—When leading and trailing edges are straight, parallel, and at right angles to the direction of flight.

(b) TAPERED—When leading and/or trailing edges are not at right angles to the direction of flight, so that wing diminishes in chord length toward the tip.

(c) ELLIPTICAL—When leading and trailing edges are elliptical in general shape.

(d) CURVED—When leading and/or trailing edge is rounded.

(e) SWEPTBACK—When the general wing shape sweeps aft toward the tips.

(f) SWEPTFORWARD—When the general wing shape sweeps forward toward the tips.

Wings are also classified by their front view shape:

a. *Horizontal*—When the wing axis forms a horizontal line.

b. *Dihedral*—When the wing axis slopes up or down from the horizontal.

c. *Gull*—When the inner panel has positive dihedral and the remainder of the wing to the tip is horizontal or has less positive dihedral.

d. *Inverted gull*—When the reverse is true, i. e., inner panel has negative dihedral and outer panel is horizontal or has positive dihedral.

Manufacturers of Foreign AIRCRAFT

BRITISH

"Airspeed"	Airspeed, Ltd.
"Armstrong Whitworth"	Sir W. G. Armstrong Whitworth Aircraft, Ltd.
"Blackburn"	The Blackburn Aircraft, Ltd.
"Boulton Paul"	Boulton Paul Aircraft, Ltd.
"Bristol"	The Bristol Aeroplane Co., Ltd.
"De Havilland"	The De Havilland Aircraft Co., Ltd.
"Fairey"	The Fairey Aviation Co., Ltd.
"Folland"	Folland Aircraft, Ltd.
"G. A."	General Aircraft, Ltd.
"Gloster"	The Gloster Aircraft Co., Ltd.
"Handley Page"	Handley Page, Ltd.
"Hawker"	Hawker Aircraft, Ltd.
"Miles"	Phillips and Powis Aircraft, Ltd.
"Percival"	Percival Aircraft, Ltd.
"Avro"	A. V. Roe and Co., Ltd.
"Saro"	Saunders-Roe, Ltd.
"Short"	Short Bros. (Rochester and Bedford) Ltd.
"Supermarine"	Supermarine Aviation Works, Div. of Vickers-Armstrongs, Ltd.
"Vickers"	Vickers-Armstrongs, Ltd.
"Westland"	Westland Aircraft, Ltd.
"Wackett"	Commonwealth Aircraft Corporation Pty., Ltd. (Australia).
"Fleet"	Fleet Aircraft, Ltd. (Canada).
"Noorduyn"	Noorduyn Aviation, Ltd. (Canada).

U. S. S. R.

State aircraft factories, grouped under control of the Central Directorate of Aeronautical Industry (Glavavioprom).

JAPAN

"Aichi"	Aichi Watcu and Electric Machinery Co., Ltd.
"Kawanishi"	Kawanishi Aircraft Co., Ltd.
"Kawasaki"	Kawasaki Aircraft Engineering Co., Ltd.
"Mitsubishi"	Mitsubishi Heavy Industries, Ltd.
"Nakajima"	Nakajima Aircraft Co., Ltd.
"Sasebo"	Sasebo Naval Arsenal.

GERMANY

"Arado"	Arado Flugzeugwerke, G. m. b. H. (Arado Aircraft Co., Ltd.).
"Blohm and Voss" (or "Ha")	Blohm und Voss
"Bücker"	Bücker Flugzeugbau, G. m. b. H. (Bücker Aircraft Co., Ltd.).
"Dornier"	Dornier-Werke, G. m. b. H. (Dornier Industries Co., Ltd.).
"Fieseler"	Gerhard Fieseler Werke, G. m. b. H. (Gerhard Fieseler Industries Co., Ltd.).
"Focke-Wulf"	Focke-Wulf Flugzeugbau, G. m. b. H. (Focke-Wulf Aircraft Co., Ltd.).
"Gotha"	Gothaer Waggonfabrik, A. G. (Gotha Vehicle Manufacturing Corp.).
"Heinkel"	Ernst Heinkel Flugzeugwerke, G. m. b. H. (Ernst Heinkel Aircraft Co., Ltd.).
"Henschel"	Henschel Flugzeugwerke, A. G. (Henschel Aircraft Corp.).
"Junkers"	Junkers Flugzeug und Motorenwerke, A. G. (Junkers Aircraft and Engine Corp.).
"Messerschmitt"	Messerschmitt, A. G. (Messerschmitt Corp.).

ITALY

"Breda"	Societa Italiana Ernesto Breda. (Ernest Breda Co. of Italy.)
"Cant"	Cantieri Riuniti dell' Adriatico. (Adriatic United Shipyards.)
"Caproni"	Aeroplani Caproni S. A. (Caproni Airplanes Co., Ltd.).
"Caproni Vizzola"	Caproni Vizzola S. A. (Caproni). (Caproni Vizzola Co., Ltd. (Caproni).)
"Fiat"	Aeronautica d'Italia S. A. (Fiat). (Italian Aircraft Co., Ltd. (Fiat).)
"Macchi"	Aeronautica Macchi S. A. (Macchi Aircraft Co., Ltd.).
"Meridionali"	S. A. Industrie Meccaniche & Aeronautiche Meridionali (Breda). (Southern Manufacturing and Aircraft Co., Ltd. (Breda).)
"Piaggio"	S. A. Piaggio & Co. (Piaggio Co., Ltd.).
"Reggiane"	Officine Meccaniche "Reggiane" S. A. (Caproni). (Reggio Manufacturing Works, Ltd. (Caproni).)
"S. A. I."	Societa Aeronautica Italiana Ing. A. Ambrosini & Co. (A. Ambrosini Aeronautical Engineering Co. of Italy).
"Savoia-Marchetti"	Societa Italiana Aeroplani Idrovolanti "Savoia-Marchetti." ("Savoia-Marchetti" Airplane and Seaplane Co. of Italy.)

NOTE: NOT ALL THESE ARE REPRESENTED IN THIS MANUAL

ARMY	NAVY AND MARINE CORPS	NAME	ORIGINAL MANUFACTURER	
B–17		Flying Fortress	Boeing	**HEAVY BOMBERS**
B–24	PB4Y	Liberator	Consolidated	
B–18		Bolo	Douglas	**MEDIUM BOMBERS**
B–23		Dragon	Douglas	
B–25	PBJ	Mitchell	North American	
B–26		Marauder	Martin	
B–34	PV	Ventura	Vega	
A–20	BD	Havoc (Attack) Boston (Bomber)	Douglas	**LIGHT BOMBERS**
A–24	SBD	Dauntless (Dive)	Douglas	
A–25	SB2C	Helldiver (Dive)	Curtiss	
A–29	PBO	Hudson (Patrol)	Lockheed	
A–34	SB2A	Buccaneer (Dive)	Brewster	
A–35, A–31		Vengeance (Dive)	Vultee	
	SB2U	Vindicator (Dive)	Chance Vought	
	TBD	Devastator (Torpedo)	Douglas	
	TBF	Avenger (Torpedo)	Grumman	
OA–10	PBY	Catalina	Consolidated	**PATROL BOMBERS (FLYING BOATS)**
	PB2Y	Coronado	Consolidated	
	PBM	Mariner	Martin	
P–38		Lightning	Lockheed	**FIGHTERS**
P–39		Airacobra	Bell	
P–40		Warhawk	Curtiss	
P–43		Lancer	Republic	
P–47		Thunderbolt	Republic	
P–51		Mustang	North American	
	F2A	Buffalo	Brewster	
	F4F	Wildcat	Grumman	
	F4U	Corsair	Chance Vought	
	F6F	Hellcat	Grumman	

NAMES of
U.S. Planes

	ARMY	NAVY AND MARINE CORPS	NAME	ORIGINAL MANUFACTURER
SCOUTING OBSERVATION (SEAPLANES)	. . . .	SO3C	Seagull	Curtiss
	. . . .	OS2U	Kingfisher	Chance Vought
TRANSPORT	C-43	GB	Traveler	Beech
	C-45A	JRB	Voyager	Beech
	C-46	R5C	Commando	Curtiss
	C-47	} R4D	} Skytrain	Douglas
	C-53		Skytrooper	Douglas
	C-54	R5D	Skymaster	Douglas
	C-60 (C-56, C-57, C-59)	R5O	Lodestar	Lockheed
	C-61	GK	Forwarder	Fairchild
	C-69	. . . . . .	Constellation	Lockheed
	C-76	. . . . . .	Caravan	Curtiss
	C-87	. . . . . .	Liberator Express	Consolidated
	. . . .	JR2S	Excalibur	Chance Vought
TRAINERS	PT-13 & 17	N2S-1 & 3 . .	Caydet	Boeing
	PT-19 & 23	. . . . . .	Cornell	Fairchild
	. . . .	N2T	Tutor	Timm
	PT-22	NR	Recruit	Ryan
	BT-13 & 15	SNV	Valiant	Vultee
	AT-6	SNJ	Texan	North American
	. . . .	SNC	Falcon	Curtiss
	AT-7	SNB-2 . . .	Navigator	Beech
	AT-8 & 17	. . . . . .	Bobcat	Cessna
	AT-10	. . . . . .	Wichita	Beech
	AT-11	SNB-1 . . .	Kansas	Beech
	AT-13 & 14	. . . . . .	Yankee-Doodle	Fairchild
	AT-15	. . . . . .	Crewmaker	Boeing
	AT-19	. . . . . .	Reliant	Vultee
LIAISON	L-1	. . . . . .	Vigilant	Vultee
	L-2	. . . . . .	Taylorcraft Grasshopper	Taylorcraft
	L-3C	. . . . . .	Aeronca Grasshopper	Aeronca
	L-4B	NE	Piper Grasshopper	Piper
	L-5	. . . . . .	Sentinel	Vultee

ARMY

The designation of Army aircraft is composed of one or two letters designating the class of aircraft, a number indicating the model and a letter to designate the modification of the model. For example the designation B–17F means that the aircraft is a bomber (B), that it is the 17th bomber model accepted by the Army, and that it is the 6th modification of the B–17 model. Unlike U. S. Navy aircraft designations, Army designations give no information as to identity of the manufacturer.

OA . . . . Amphibian . . . .
F . . . . Army Reconnaissance (Photographic)
A . . . . Bombardment (Light)
B . . . . Bombardment (Medium and Heavy)
P . . . . Fighter
L . . . . Liaison
O . . . . Observation
AT . . . . Training (Advance)
BT . . . . Training (Basic)
PT . . . . Training (Primary)
C . . . . Transport (Cargo and Personnel)
UC . . . . Utility Transport (Less than 9 places or less than 1,400 lbs. of cargo)
CG . . . . Glider (Troop)
TG . . . . Glider (Training)
CQ . . . . Target (Control)
OQ . . . . Target (Aerial)
PQ . . . . Target (Aerial)

Classifications are prefixed as follows:

R . . . . Restricted Classification (Planes no longer considered as First Line aircraft)
X . . . . Experimental Classification
Y . . . . Service Test Classification
Z . . . . Obsolete Classification

NAVY

The designation of Navy airplanes, airships, and gliders is composed of one or two letters designating the class of aircraft; a number indicating the model; a letter indicating the manufacturer; and a number to designate the modifications of the model. As an example, the first patrol bombing aeroplane to be produced by Consolidated Aircraft would be the PBY–1. The modifications to this aircraft would be the PBY–2, PBY–3, etc. The second patrol bombing aeroplane built by this company would be the PB2Y–1 and successive modifications to this aeroplane would be the PB2Y–2, PB2Y–3, etc. The prefix letter "X" is used for experimental aircraft and gliders.

H . . . . Ambulance
B . . . . Bombing
F . . . . Fighting
O . . . . Observation
P . . . . Patrol
S . . . . Scouting
T . . . . Torpedo
OS . . . . Observation-Scouting
N . . . . Training
R . . . . Transport (multi-engine)
G . . . . Transport (single-engine)
J . . . . Utility
BT . . . . Bombing Torpedo
PB . . . . Patrol-Bombing
SB . . . . Scouting-Bombing
JR . . . . Utility-Transport
L . . . . Glider
ZN . . . . Airship (nonrigid)
SO . . . . Scouting-Observatio
SN . . . . Scout-Training
TB . . . . Torpedo-Bombing

CURRENT NAVY MANUFACTURER'S LETTERS

A Brewster Aeronautical Corp.

Allied Aviation Corp.

B Beech Aircraft Co.

Boeing Aircraft Co.

Budd Manufacturing Co.

C Curtiss Airplane Div. (C-W Corp.)

D Douglas Aircraft Co., Inc.

E Bellanca Aircraft Corp.

Gould Aeronautical Corp.

Piper Aircraft Co.

F Grumman Aircraft Eng. Corp.

Columbia Aircraft Corp.

Fairchild Aircraft Corp. (Canada).

G AGA Aviation Corp.

Goodyear Aircraft Corp.

Great Lakes Aircraft Co.

H Howard Aircraft Co.

Hall Aluminum Co.

J North American Aviation.

K Fairchild Aircraft Corp. (U. S.)

Nash-Kelvinator Co.

L Bell Aircraft Corp.

Langley Aviation Corp.

M Glenn L. Martin Co.

General Motors Corp., Eastern Aircraft Division.

N Naval Aircraft Factory

O Lockheed Aircraft Corp.

P Spartan Aircraft Co.

Q Bristol Aeronautical Corp.

R Ryan Aeronautical Co.

Aeronca Aircraft Corp.

S Sikorsky Aircraft

Stearman Aircraft (Division of Boeing Aircraft Co.)

Schweizer Aircraft

T El Segundo Plant (Douglas Aircraft Co.)

Taylorcraft Aviation Corp.

Northrop Aircraft, Inc.

Timm Aircraft Corp.

U Chance Vought Aircraft (Div. United Aircraft Corp.) (formerly Vought-Sikorsky)

V Vultee Aircraft Inc.

Vickers Ltd.

Vega Airplane Co.

W Canadian Car & Foundry.

Waco Aircraft Co.

Y Consolidated Aircraft Corp.

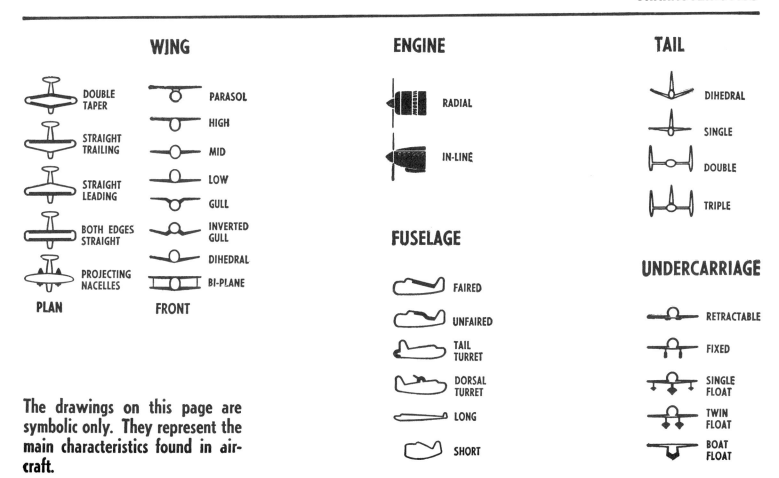

WING

PLAN		FRONT	
	DOUBLE TAPER		PARASOL
	STRAIGHT TRAILING		HIGH
	STRAIGHT LEADING		MID
	BOTH EDGES STRAIGHT		LOW
	PROJECTING NACELLES		GULL
			INVERTED GULL
			DIHEDRAL
			BI-PLANE

ENGINE

RADIAL

IN-LINE

FUSELAGE

FAIRED

UNFAIRED

TAIL TURRET

DORSAL TURRET

LONG

SHORT

TAIL

DIHEDRAL

SINGLE

DOUBLE

TRIPLE

UNDERCARRIAGE

RETRACTABLE

FIXED

SINGLE FLOAT

TWIN FLOAT

BOAT FLOAT

The drawings on this page are symbolic only. They represent the main characteristics found in aircraft.

ARMY: **P-38E**
P-38 series
F-4, F-5

R. A. F.: LIGHTNING I, II

FIGHTER

U.S.A.   **U.K.**

P-38 "LIGHTNING"

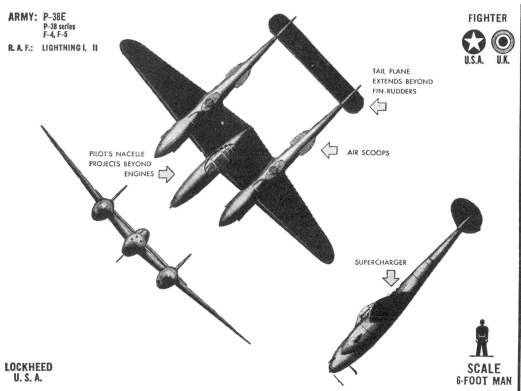

TAIL PLANE
EXTENDS BEYOND
FIN-RUDDERS

AIR SCOOPS

PILOT'S NACELLE
PROJECTS BEYOND
ENGINES

SUPERCHARGER

SCALE
6-FOOT MAN

LOCKHEED
U. S. A.

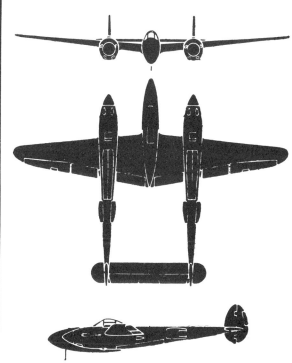

DISTINGUISHING FEATURES: Twin-engine, mid-wing monoplane. Pilot's central nacelle projects well forward to rounded nose. Sharper taper on trailing edge of wings. Full dihedral from the roots. In-line engines mounted in nacelles at forward ends of twin tail booms extending from motors to stabilizer. Air scoops for radiators fitted on sides of booms halfway back. Stabilizer is long and rectangular with rounded tips extending outboard of the booms. Twin fins and rudders are egg-shaped.

APRIL 1943
FROM DATA CURRENTLY AVAILABLE

INTEREST: In addition to speed, range, and excellent high altitude performance, versatility is an outstanding characteristic of this aircraft. In the Aleutians, in the South Pacific, in Europe and in North Africa, it has been in use both as a low and high altitude fighter and as a photographic reconnaissance aircraft (in latter case, designated as F-4 and F-5). The fact that its propellers rotate in opposite directions, thus balancing torque, enhances maneuverability of the P-38. With its twin tail booms, the Lightning is one of the easiest aircraft to recognize.

WAR DEPARTMENT FM 30—30
NAVY DEPARTMENT BUAER 3

SPAN: 52 ft.
LENGTH: 37 ft. 10 in.
APPROX. MAX. SPEED: over 400 m. p. h.

SERVICE CEILING:
over 30,000 ft.

RESTRICTED

ARMY: P-39E
P-39 series

R.A.F.: AIRACOBRA I

FIGHTER

U.S.A.   U.K.

P-39 "AIRACOBRA"

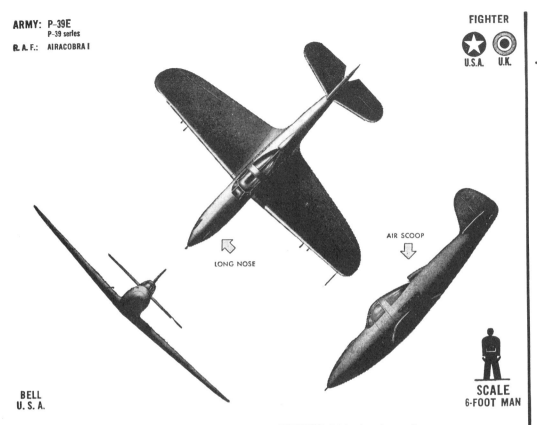

LONG NOSE

AIR SCOOP

BELL
U.S.A.

SCALE
6-FOOT MAN

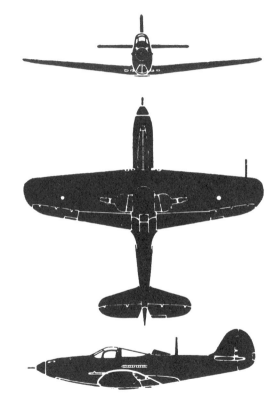

DISTINGUISHING FEATURES: Low-wing monoplane with dihedral from wing roots. Wing is set midship. Slight taper on leading edge and sharper taper on trailing edge. Long thin nose covering cannon which fires through spinner. Airscoop is directly behind pilot. Long slim fuselage. Small fin and rudder with tapered leading edge and rounded trailing edge. Entire fuselage is curved giving plane a graceful rocker effect.

INTEREST: This aircraft, rated among the most graceful airplanes in the air today, often mounts a 37-mm cannon, the heaviest carried by any aircraft of similar type. The P-39 has been used effectively for ground strafing, and as a low altitude fighter. Heavy defensive armor protects the pilot against ground fire when operating at low altitudes. The engine is placed amidship in the fuselage behind the pilot's cockpit, the propeller being driven by a 10-foot shaft.

SPAN: 34 ft.
LENGTH: 30 ft. 2 in.
APPROX. MAX. SPEED: over 360 m. p. h.

SERVICE CEILING:
over 30,000 ft.

APRIL 1943
FROM DATA CURRENTLY AVAILABLE

WAR DEPARTMENT FM 30—30
NAVY DEPARTMENT BUAER 3

RESTRICTED

ARMY: **P-40F**
P-40 series

R. A. F.: WARHAWK
KITTYHAWK I, II, III
TOMAHAWK I, II

RUSSIA, N. E. L, CHINA

FIGHTER

U.S.A. U.K. U.S.S.R

CHINA FRANCE

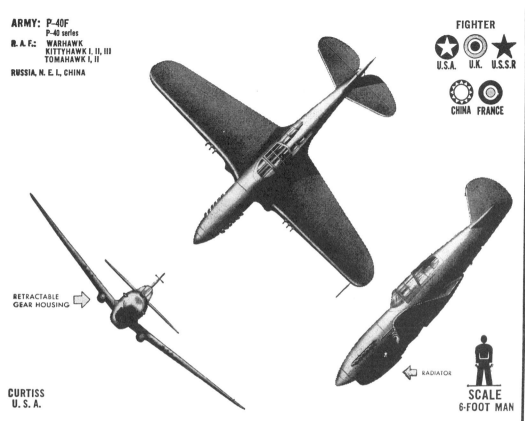

RETRACTABLE
GEAR HOUSING ⇨

**CURTISS
U. S. A.**

← RADIATOR

**SCALE
6-FOOT MAN**

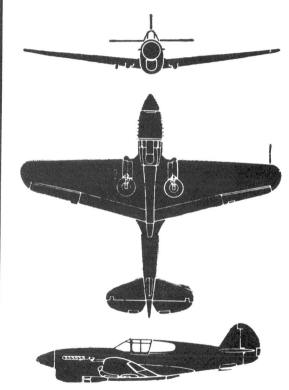

DISTINGUISHING FEATURES: Single-engine, low-wing monoplane. Wings have full dihedral showing prominent landing gear knuckles close to fuselage on lower surface. Leading edge nearly straight. Trailing edge has pronounced taper. In-line engine with deep radiator under long nose. Large spinner is set flush with cowling. Rounded fin and rudder. Large "cut-out" in elevators.

INTEREST: This is one of the best known and most widely used American fighters. Earlier models, called "Tomahawks" and "Kittyhawks" by the British were used in Libya, on the Russian front, and by the "Flying Tigers" in China. The Warhawk is the first American aircraft to be equipped with the famous Merlin engine. This fighter has excellent armor, high diving speed, good maneuverability, and heavy hitting power. Although the P-40 is not at its best in higher altitudes, it is one of the most versatile of aircraft.

SPAN: 37 ft. 4 in.
LENGTH: 31 ft. 9 in.
APPROX. MAX. SPEED: 360 m. p. h.

SERVICE CEILING:
over 30,000 ft.

APRIL 1943
FROM DATA CURRENTLY AVAILABLE

WAR DEPARTMENT FM 30-30
NAVY DEPARTMENT BUAER 3

RESTRICTED

ARMY: P-47D
P-47 series

R. A. F.: THUNDERBOLT

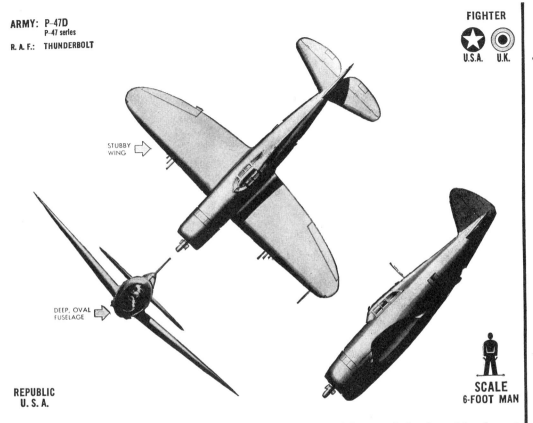

STUBBY WING ⇨

DEEP, OVAL FUSELAGE ⇨

REPUBLIC U.S.A.

SCALE 6-FOOT MAN

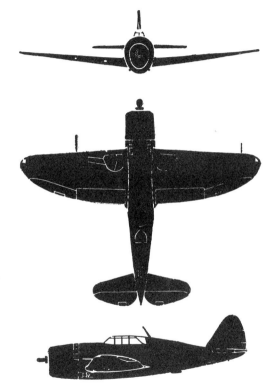

DISTINGUISHING FEATURES: Low mid-wing monoplane with single radial engine. Wing has slightly tapered edge and semi-elliptical trailing edge. Wings have full dihedral from roots. Engine cowl is oval-shaped with propeller hub set above center. Fuselage has thick heavy appearance with sharp ridge down sloping back. Single fin and rudder with pronounced taper on leading edge and curved trailing edge.

INTEREST: The P-47 is one of the largest and fastest single engine fighters yet built. Its weight of over 5 tons, with nearly a ton of guns and ammunition, is greater than that of many commercial transports of a few years ago. Designed in 1941, this was the highest horsepower single engine fighter yet produced for the Army Air Forces. Use of a four-blade propeller reduces the size of the propeller arc, while still coping with the engine's great power output. This aircraft was designed for fighting at high altitudes.

SPAN: 40 ft. 10 in.
LENGTH: 35 ft. 4 in.
APPROX. MAX. SPEED: over 390 m. p. h.

SERVICE CEILING: over 38,000 ft.

RESTRICTED

ARMY: P–51
P–51 series
A–36

R. A. F.   MUSTANG I

FIGHTER

U.S.A.   U.K.

P-51 "MUSTANG"

SQUARE TIPS
ON WING &
STABILIZER

SQUARE
TAIL

RADIATOR

NOTE SIMILARITY TO Me109

NORTH AMERICAN
U. S. A.

SCALE
6-FOOT MAN

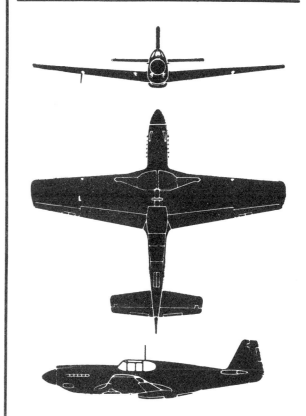

DISTINGUISHING FEATURES: Single in-line engine low-wing monoplane with long pointed nose. Wings have full dihedral and are tapered to nearly square tips. Long radiator mounted under fuselage extends aft of cockpit enclosure. Single fin and rudder is tall with a square top.

INTEREST: The Mustang was developed quietly and attracted little public notice until used by the British during the dramatic Commando raid on Dieppe. Although this aircraft has been used on fighter sweeps over Europe, a large part of its job in the war may prove to be that of strafing and reconnaissance. In this capacity it is joining the Tomahawk (P–40) and the Lysander in British Army cooperation squadrons. An outstanding virtue of this aircraft is its speed near the ground. A bomber version fitted with dive brakes, the A–36, is now in service for ground-air support.

SPAN: 37 ft.
LENGTH: 32 ft. 3 in.
APPROX. MAX. SPEED: 390 m. p. h

SERVICE CEILING:
over 30,000 ft.

APRIL 1943
FROM DATA CURRENTLY AVAILABLE

WAR DEPARTMENT FM 30–30
NAVY DEPARTMENT BUAER 3

RESTRICTED

ARMY: A-20A
A-20 series; P-70

R.A.F.: BOSTON I, II, III
HAVOC I, II

NAVY: BD-2

FRANCE: DB-7B

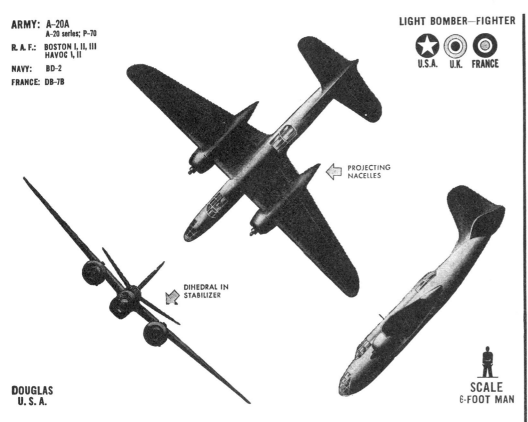

PROJECTING NACELLES

DIHEDRAL IN STABILIZER

DOUGLAS
U. S. A.

SCALE
6-FOOT MAN

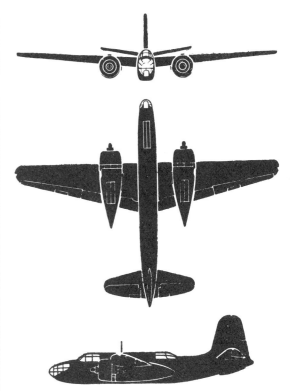

DISTINGUISHING FEATURES: Shoulder wing monoplane with long thin transparent nose. Wing has straight leading edge and pronounced taper to trailing edge. Twin radial engines are underslung with nacelles extending well beyond the trailing edge of wing. Fuselage has a graceful attitude due to the turned up after section. Tall single fin and rudder.

INTEREST: This aircraft is unquestionably one of the best in its class. Designed as a fast day bomber, this plane is also used as a fighter. The night fighter version with solid nose is known as the P-70, while the British know the A-20 as the "Boston" when used as a bomber and as the "Havoc" when used for ground attack. The U. S. Navy designation is BD. The A-20 is much used in large scale daylight fighter and bomber sweeps over France and in North Africa. Because of its high performance, striking power and maneuverability, losses have been relatively small.

SPAN: 61 ft. 4 in.
LENGTH: 48 ft.
APPROX. SPEED: 340 m. p. h.

SERVICE CEILING: over 24,000 ft.

ARMY: A-29
A-29, A; A-28, A
AT-18

R. A. F.: HUDSON I to VI

NAVY: PBO-1

N. E. I., CHINA

LIGHT BOMBER

U.S.A.   U.K.   CHINA

RUDDERS INSET
ON TAIL PLANE

FOWLER FLAP TRACKS

LONG DEEP NOSE

PRONOUNCED
DIHEDRAL

DORSAL TURRET

**LOCKHEED
U. S. A.**

SCALE
6-FOOT MAN

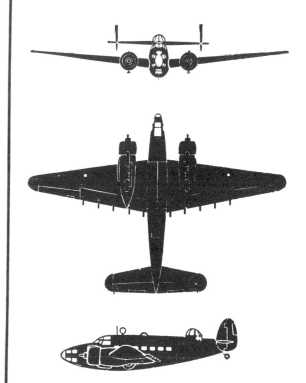

DISTINGUISHING FEATURES: Two-engine mid-wing monoplane. Wings taper equally to sharp rounded tips and have full dihedral. Fowler flap guides project beyond trailing edge of wing. Fuselage is short and deep with pointed transparent nose. Large dorsal turret well aft. Oval twin fins and rudders set inboard.

INTEREST: The British have called this aircraft the "Old Boomerang" because it "always comes back." It was the first American-built type to be flown across the Atlantic to England by Ferry Command pilots. The prototype which first flew in 1939 was developed from a Lockheed commercial transport. Considered by the British to be one of the air achievements of the war, the Hudson is now sharing service with the newer and larger "Ventura."

SPAN: 65 ft. 6 in.
LENGTH: 44 ft. 3 in.
APPROX. MAX. SPEED: 265 m. p. h.

SERVICE CEILING:
over 25,000 ft.

**APRIL 1943
FROM DATA CURRENTLY AVAILABLE**

WAR DEPARTMENT FM 30—30
NAVY DEPARTMENT BUAER 3

RESTRICTED

ARMY: A-30
R.A.F.: BALTIMORE I, II, III

LIGHT BOMBER

U.S.A.   U.K.

A-30 "BALTIMORE"

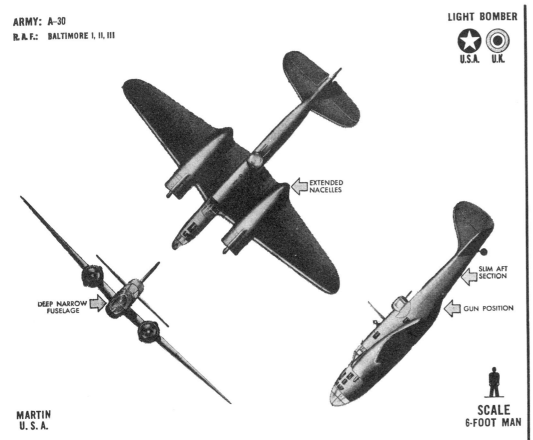

EXTENDED NACELLES

DEEP NARROW FUSELAGE

SLIM AFT SECTION

GUN POSITION

MARTIN
U. S. A.

SCALE
6-FOOT MAN

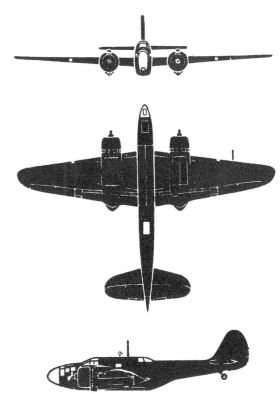

DISTINGUISHING FEATURES: Mid-wing monoplane with two radial engines. Deep, narrow fuselage with deep step on underside aft of the wing. Transparent plastic nose. Rounded single fin and rudder.
INTEREST: Although designed primarily as a light bomber, this aircraft is also well-suited for long-range reconnaissance. Its speed, defensive armament, and maneuverability make it capable of dealing effectively with enemy fighter planes. Developed from the lighter Maryland to meet specific needs of the R. A. F., it ranks as one of the highest climbing, and one of the fastest of its type. Early models do not have a top turret. Thus far, it has been in operational service almost exclusively with the Royal Air Force in the Middle East.

SPAN: 61 ft. 4 in.
LENGTH: 48 ft. 6 in.
APPROX. MAX. SPEED: 315 m. p. h.

SERVICE CEILING:
over 22,000 ft.

RESTRICTED

ARMY: A–35 (A–31)
    A–35, A B; A–31 C

R. A. F.: VENGEANCE I

CHINA

DIVE BOMBER

U.S.A.   U.K.   CHINA

A-35 (A-31) "VENGEANCE"

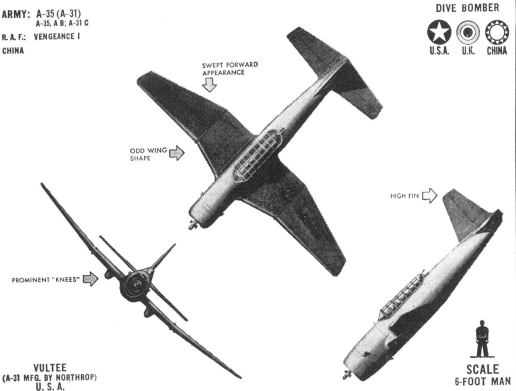

SWEPT FORWARD
APPEARANCE

ODD WING
SHAPE

HIGH FIN

PROMINENT "KNEES"

VULTEE
(A-31 MFG. BY NORTHROP)
U. S. A.

SCALE
6-FOOT MAN

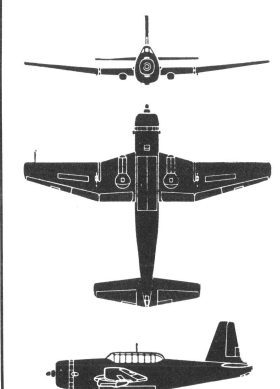

DISTINGUISHING FEATURES: Mid-wing monoplane with single radial engine. Center section of wing has swept-back leading edge and straight trailing edge. Outer sections have straight leading edge and sharply tapered trailing edge with blunt tips. Prominent knuckles show at under-carriage attachment. Cockpit enclosure is long and horizontal. Very high triangular fin and rudder with square top.

INTEREST: The British ordered this very maneuverable

two-place dive bomber in July 1940, just after the German Ju 87–B (Stuka) had figured so prominently in the defeat of France. However, since that time, it has been shown that in land warfare, dive bombers are extremely vulnerable in face of adequate fighter opposition and well organized anti-aircraft fire. It is therefore more likely that the Vengeance will be used for general reconnaissance purposes except where local conditions favor dive bombing. A modified version is coming into use by the U. S. Navy as the TBV–1.

SPAN: 48 ft.
LENGTH: 40 ft.
APPROX. MAX. SPEED: over 280 m. p. h.

SERVICE CEILING:
over 20,000 ft.

RESTRICTED

APRIL 1943
FROM DATA CURRENTLY AVAILABLE

WAR DEPARTMENT FM 30–30
NAVY DEPARTMENT BUAER 3

ARMY: **B-17E**
B-17 series

R. A. F.: **FORTRESS I, II SUPER-FLYING FORTRESS**

U.S.A.   **U.K.**

B-17 "FLYING FORTRESS"

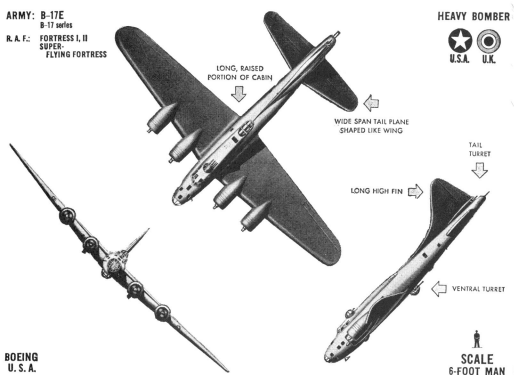

LONG, RAISED PORTION OF CABIN

WIDE SPAN TAIL PLANE SHAPED LIKE WING

TAIL TURRET

LONG HIGH FIN

VENTRAL TURRET

BOEING U.S.A.

SCALE 6-FOOT MAN

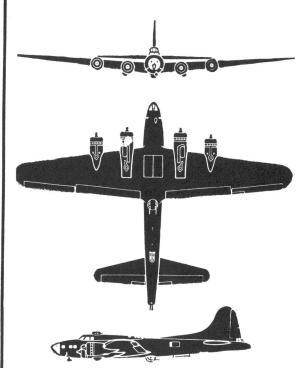

DISTINGUISHING FEATURES: Four-engine, low-wing monoplane. Wings equally tapered with rounded tips and full dihedral. Long, narrow fuselage. Gun turret on top of fuselage just aft of pilot's cockpit enclosure. Large ventral turret aft of wings. Tail has broad single fin and rudder with fin faired far forward into fuselage. Large stabilizer and elevator, similar in shape to the wing.

INTEREST: Designed for high altitude, daytime precision bombing of restricted targets, the B-17 was the first long-range American bomber. Intended primarily

for long flights over the Pacific, great fuel capacity rather than tremendous bomb load was emphasized in the individual design. It now does effective work, however, for the Army Air Forces in raids at shorter range in Europe, North Africa, and in the Southwest Pacific. The relative lack of armament characterizing early models is now corrected so it is possible on some missions to operate under the protection of its own guns without fighter escort. The early models, B-17 to B-17D had a much smaller fin with straight leading edge intersecting the fuselage back of the L. E. of the stabilizer.

SPAN: 103 ft. 10 in.
LENGTH: 74 ft. 9 in.
APPROX. MAX. SPEED: 310 m. p. h.

SERVICE CEILING: over 35,000 ft.

APRIL 1943
FROM DATA CURRENTLY AVAILABLE

WAR DEPARTMENT FM 30—30
NAVY DEPARTMENT BUAER 3

ARMY: B-24E
B-24 series
C-87

R.A.F.: LIBERATOR I to IV

NAVY: PB4Y-1

B-24 "LIBERATOR"

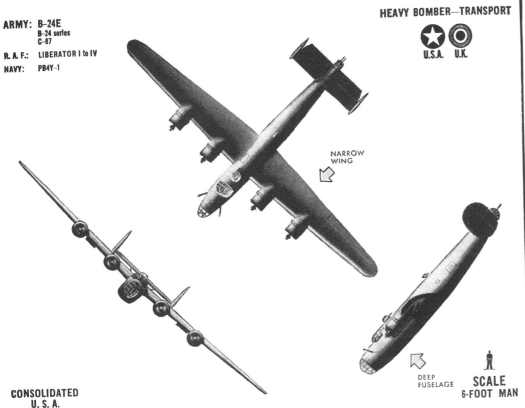

NARROW WING

DEEP FUSELAGE

SCALE 6-FOOT MAN

CONSOLIDATED
U. S. A.

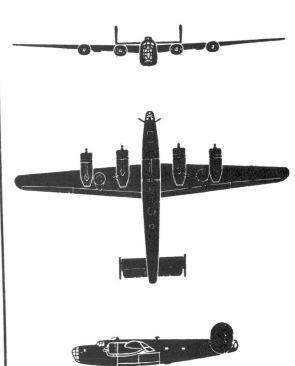

DISTINGUISHING FEATURES: High mid-wing monoplane. Four radial engines. Long narrow equally tapered wings with small rounded tips and slight dihedral. Deep bulky fuselage. Large rounded twin fins and rudders set flush with outer end of stabilizer.

INTEREST: This long-range bomber is used in all theaters by the British and the U. S. Army Air Forces. It has high speed, powerful armaments and is extremely maneuverable for its size. All of these factors reduce the number of fighter craft required for its protection. The B-24's high performance results in part from its clean design and use of the thin "Davis" wing which materially reduces drag. The military transport version, designated as the C-87, has a nontransparent nose, and a cabin under the wing in place of the bomb bay. It was this aircraft which carried Mr. Willkie on his round-the-world mission in the autumn of 1942.

SPAN: 110 ft.
LENGTH: 66 ft.
APPROX. MAX. SPEED: 310 m. p. h.

SERVICE CEILING: over 30,000 ft.

RESTRICTED

APRIL 1943
FROM DATA CURRENTLY AVAILABLE

WAR DEPARTMENT FM 30-30
NAVY DEPARTMENT BUAER 3

ARMY: B-25 C
B-25 series
NAVY: PBJ
R. A. F.: MITCHELL I, II, III

MEDIUM BOMBER

U.S.A. **U.K.**

B-25 "MITCHELL"

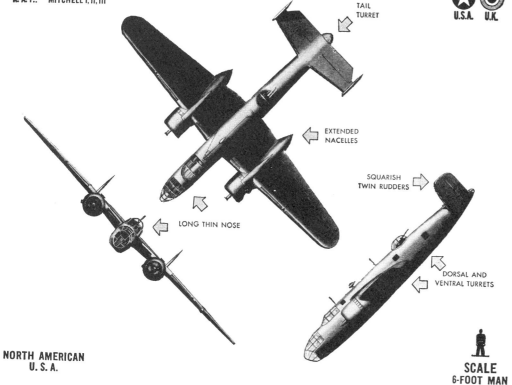

TAIL
TURRET

EXTENDED
NACELLES

SQUARISH
TWIN RUDDERS

LONG THIN NOSE

DORSAL AND
VENTRAL TURRETS

**NORTH AMERICAN
U. S. A.**

**SCALE
6-FOOT MAN**

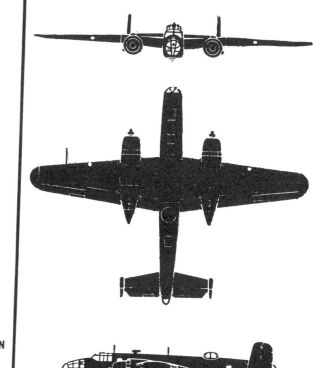

DISTINGUISHING FEATURES: Two radial engines underslung below wings. Nacelles extend beyond trailing edge of wing. High outboard twin fins and rudders sloped like a lopsided rectangle. Gull wing effect due to positive dihedral on inboard panel only. Wings tapered on both edges with more pronounced taper on trailing edge. Long transparent nose.

APRIL 1943
FROM DATA CURRENTLY AVAILABLE

INTEREST: The B-25 was named after the late Gen. "Billy" Mitchell. It has gained considerable publicity as the result of its use in the bombing raid on Tokyo in April 1942. It is in use on nearly all of the Allied war fronts and has performed well for the British in their African campaigns.

WAR DEPARTMENT FM 30–30
NAVY DEPARTMENT BUAER 3

SPAN: 67 ft. 6 in.
LENGTH: 54 ft. 1 in.
APPROX. MAX. SPEED: 300 m. p. h.

SERVICE CEILING:
25,000 ft.

RESTRICTED

ARMY: **B-26B, C**
B-26 series

R. A. F.: **MARAUDER I, II**

U.S.A. **U.K.**

B-26 "MARAUDER"

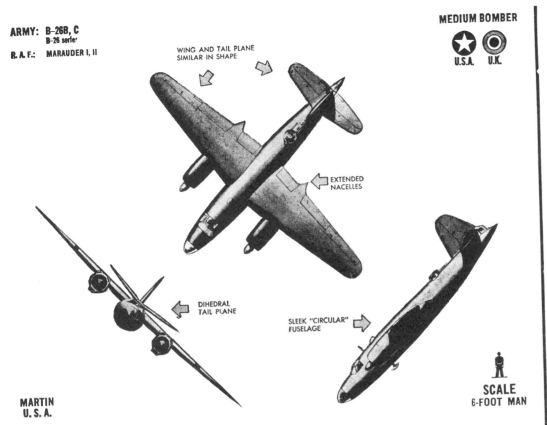

WING AND TAIL PLANE
SIMILAR IN SHAPE

EXTENDED
NACELLES

DIHEDRAL
TAIL PLANE

SLEEK "CIRCULAR"
FUSELAGE

SCALE
6-FOOT MAN

**MARTIN
U.S.A.**

DISTINGUISHING FEATURES: Shoulder wing monoplane with long cigar-shaped fuselage. Sharply tapered wings with rounded tips and no dihedral. High single fin and rudder with rounded top. Tail plane has marked dihedral. Radial engines underslung beneath wings with long nacelles projecting beyond trailing edge. Rear fuselage fairing projects downward and beyond the tail assembly.

INTEREST: No Axis aircraft of the same class matches the B-26 for speed, range, or bomb-carrying capacity. In the Battle of Midway, it was used as a torpedo bomber—the first time that land-based torpedo bombers of the U. S. Army had been in action. One of them came back with over 500 bullet holes in fuselage and wings. The design for this aircraft was completely new and owes little to any previous conception. The early models, the B-26 and B-26A, had a wing span of 65 feet.

SPAN: 71 ft.
LENGTH: 58 ft. 3 in.
APPROX. MAX. SPEED: over 300 m. p. h.

SERVICE CEILING:
over 23,000 ft.

RESTRICTED

ARMY: C-46
C-46 A

NAVY: R5C-1

RAF: COMMANDO

TRANSPORT—GLIDER TUG

U.S.A. U.K.

C-46 "COMMANDO"

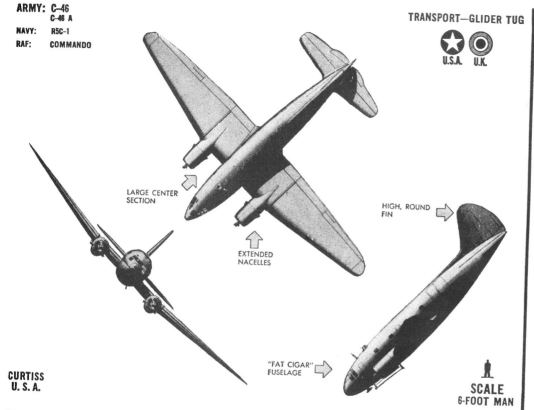

LARGE CENTER SECTION

EXTENDED NACELLES

HIGH, ROUND FIN

"FAT CIGAR" FUSELAGE

SCALE
6-FOOT MAN

CURTISS U.S.A.

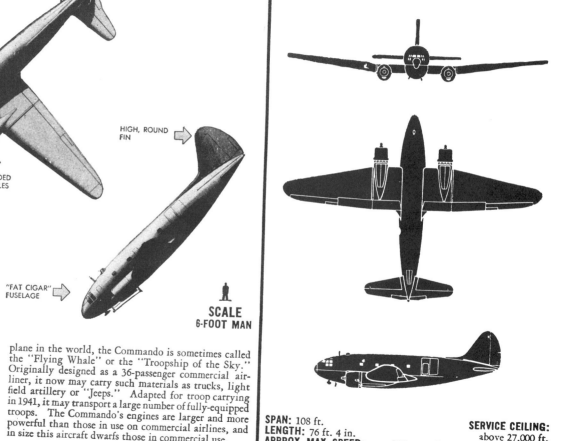

DISTINGUISHING FEATURES: Low mid-wing monoplane with two radial engines. Wings tapered on outer panels with most of the taper on leading edges. Engines slightly underslung, projecting well forward of wing. Fuselage is cylindrical in shape with pointed nose unbroken by step for cockpit enclosure. Rounded single fin and rudder sweeping into fuselage.

INTEREST: The largest twin-engined military cargo

APRIL 1943
FROM DATA CURRENTLY AVAILABLE

plane in the world, the Commando is sometimes called the "Flying Whale" or the "Troopship of the Sky." Originally designed as a 36-passenger commercial airliner, it now may carry such materials as trucks, light field artillery or "Jeeps." Adapted for troop carrying in 1941, it may transport a large number of fully-equipped troops. The Commando's engines are larger and more powerful than those in use on commercial airlines, and in size this aircraft dwarfs those in commercial use.

WAR DEPARTMENT FM 30—30
NAVY DEPARTMENT BUAER 3

SPAN: 108 ft.
LENGTH: 76 ft. 4 in.
APPROX. MAX. SPEED: over 260 m. p. h.

SERVICE CEILING: above 27,000 ft.

RESTRICTED

C-47 "SKYTRAIN"
C-53 "SKYTROOPER"

ARMY: C-47
C-47 to C-53
NAVY: R4D-1, 2, 3, 4
COMMERCIAL: DC-3
R. A. F.: DAKOTA I, II
RUSSIA: PS-84
N. E. I., CHINA

TRANSPORT—GLIDER TUG

U.S.A. U.K.

CHINA U.S.S.R.

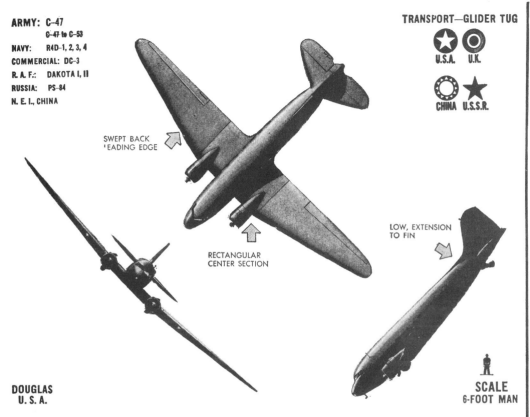

SWEPT BACK LEADING EDGE

RECTANGULAR CENTER SECTION

LOW, EXTENSION TO FIN

SCALE
6-FOOT MAN

DOUGLAS
U. S. A.

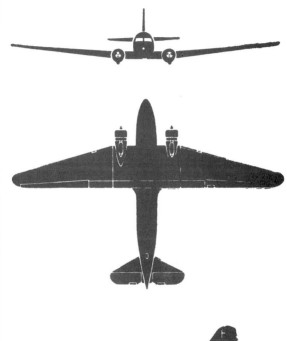

DISTINGUISHING FEATURES: Twin-engine low-wing monoplane. Center section of wing has no dihedral. Outer section of leading edge has sharp taper. Trailing edge is straight and tips are sharply rounded. The tail fin is faired forward for about one-third the length of the fuselage. The tail plane is sharply tapered at the leading edge.

INTEREST: This troop and cargo transport is the military transport version of the DC-3, one of the best-known and most widely used American commercial aircraft. The C-47 is built under license in Russia and designated the PS-84. It is used as a standard transport of the Russian Air Force. This aircraft is designated as either the C-47 or the C-53, depending on the internal arrangement and use of cargo and jumping hatches. The name "Skytrain" comes from use of this transport as a troop carrier and as a glider tug. In England it is known as the Dakota.

SPAN: 95 ft.
LENGTH: 64 ft. 6 in.
APPROX. MAX. SPEED: 220 m. p. h.

SERVICE CEILING:
24,000 ft.

APRIL 1943
FROM DATA CURRENTLY AVAILABLE

WAR DEPARTMENT FM 30—30
NAVY DEPARTMENT BUAER 3

RESTRICTED

ARMY: C-54
C-54, A
NAVY: R5D-1
COMMERCIAL: DC-4

TRANSPORT

U.S.A.

C-54 "SKYMASTER"

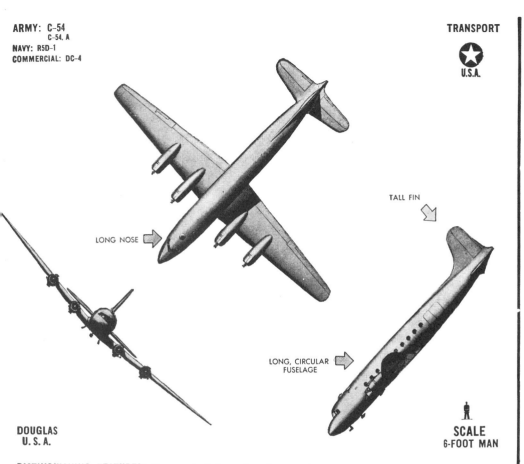

LONG NOSE

TALL FIN

LONG, CIRCULAR FUSELAGE

DOUGLAS
U. S. A.

SCALE
6-FOOT MAN

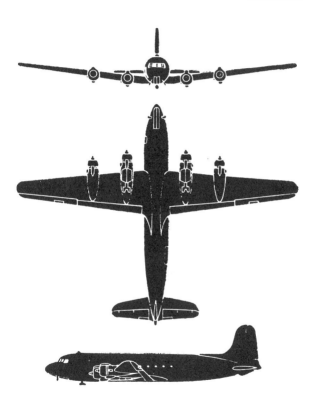

DISTINGUISHING FEATURES: Four-engined low-wing monoplane. Narrow, equally tapered wings with small rounded tips. Thick fuselage with long massive nose. Tall fin and rudder faired into fuselage.
INTEREST: This troop and cargo carrier is the largest operational military transport aircraft in the United States today. Its commercial designation was DC-4, the prototype of which was sold to Japan. The current military version differs in many ways, however, from the plane which the Japanese purchased. As a troop transport, the Skymaster can carry more than 40 fully equipped soldiers.

SPAN: 117 ft. 6 in.
LENGTH: 93 ft. 10 in.
APPROX. MAX. SPEED: over 280 m. p. h.

SERVICE CEILING:
over 22,200 ft.

APRIL 1943
FROM DATA CURRENTLY AVAILABLE

WAR DEPARTMENT FM 30—30
NAVY DEPARTMENT BUAER 3

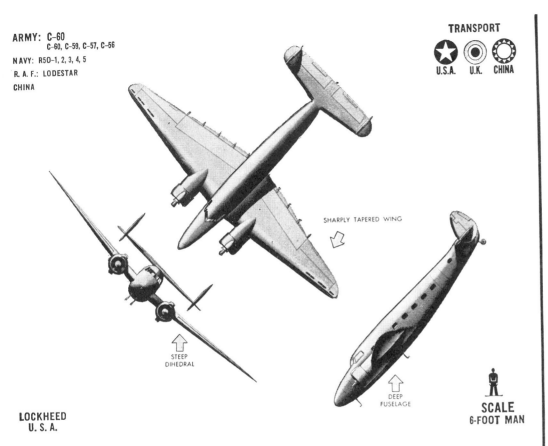

ARMY: **C-60**
C-60, C-59, C-57, C-56

NAVY: R5O-1, 2, 3, 4, 5

R. A. F.: LODESTAR

CHINA

LOCKHEED
U. S. A.

SHARPLY TAPERED WING

STEEP
DIHEDRAL

DEEP
FUSELAGE

SCALE
6-FOOT MAN

DISTINGUISHING FEATURES: Two engined low mid-wing monoplane with full dihedral. Wings have pronounced taper to sharply rounded tips. Fowler flap guides prominent at trailing edge. Deep fuselage with sharply rounded nose. Egg shaped twin fins and rudders are set inboard.

INTEREST: This aircraft is the military version of the world's fastest commercial transport. It was first converted to military use in order to convey parachute troops for the Netherlands East Indies government. Alternate designations of the Lodestar are C-56, C-57, C-59, depending on the interior equipment. The Hudson (A-29) was developed from the commercial version of this aircraft.

C-60 "LODESTAR"

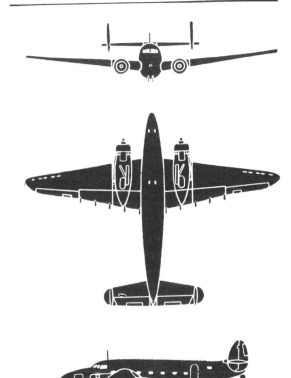

SPAN: 65 ft. 8 in.
LENGTH: 49 ft. 10 in.
APPROX. MAX. SPEED: 265 m. p. h.

SERVICE CEILING:
30,000 ft.

RESTRICTED

TRANSPORT
ADVANCED TRAINER

U.S.A.   U.K.

BOBCAT, UC-78; AT-17

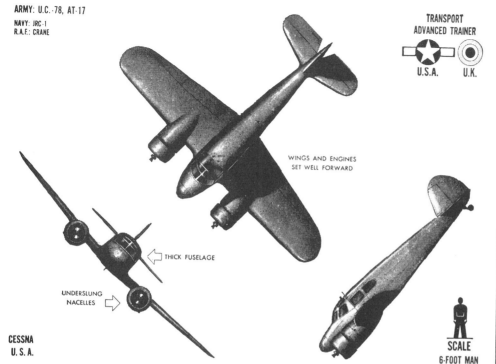

WINGS AND ENGINES
SET WELL FORWARD

THICK FUSELAGE

UNDERSLUNG
NACELLES

CESSNA
U. S. A.

SCALE
6-FOOT MAN

DISTINGUISHING FEATURES: Twin radial engine, low-wing monoplane. Moderate taper to wings. Rounded tips. Engines are underslung. Short-nose fuselage has large faired cabin and tapers sharply rearward. Bell-shaped single fin and rudder. Taper on leading edge of tailplane only.

INTEREST: The Bobcat has been used as an advanced trainer under the Joint Air Training Plan. It differs only slightly from the Cessna T–50 five-seat commercial cabin plane. It is used by the USAAF as a light transport under the designation of UC–78. As a trainer it is known as the AT–17. This aircraft is also used by the Royal Canadian Air Force, where it is referred to as the Crane. Both Canadian and U.S. models are fitted with two 225-hp. Jacobs radial engines.

SPAN: 41 ft. 11 in. **SERVICE CEILING:**
LENGTH: 32 ft. 9 in.
MAX. SPEED: 195 m. p. h. at Sea Level

NAVIGATOR AT-7, 11

DISTINGUISHING FEATURES: Single radial engine, low-wing monoplane. Wings have equal taper with round tips. Long, prominent cockpit canopy. Fuselage bulges down beneath wing and nose extends well forward. Fixed, single-strut landing gear near leading edge of wing. High, narrow, triangular fin and rudder with round top. Tapered tailplane with round tips.

INTEREST: The Valiant is the latest in a long series of Vultee-built basic trainers. Powered with a 450-hp. radial engine and weighing over 4,000 lb., this basic trainer gives the student his first instruction on a heavier low-wing type. The power, speed, and general performance are such that the step from basic to advanced military types is not drastic. It has made a fine contribution in the training of a vast number of Allied pilots.

VALIANT BT-13, BT-15; SNV-1, 2

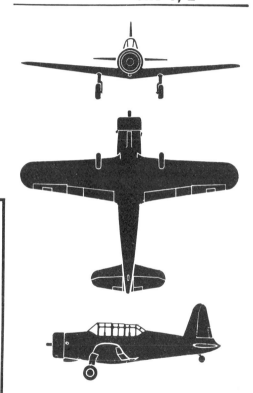

DISTINGUISHING FEATURES: Twin radial engine low-wing monoplane. Tapered wings with round tips and more pronounced taper on leading edge. Wide cabin-type fuselage with marked taper aft of wing. Twin outboard fins and rudders with rounded trailing edges and V-shaped leading edges. Tailplane has tapered leading edge and straight trailing edge.

INTEREST: This navigational trainer, designated SNB–2 by the Navy, is equipped for simultaneous training of three student navigators in celestial, dead reckoning, and radio navigation. The bomber trainer version, the AT–11 Kansas (Navy SNB–1), has a blunt glazed nose for a student bombardier. This versatile Beechcraft plane is also used as a light transport and for photographic work, designated respectively the C–45 Voyager (Navy JRB) and the F–2.

SPAN: 47 ft. 8 in.　　**SERVICE CEILING:**
LENGTH: 34 ft. 3 in.
APPROX. SPEED: 224 m. p. h. at 5,000 ft.

SPAN: 42 ft.　　**SERVICE CEILING:**
LENGTH: 28 ft. 7 in.
MAX. SPEED: 166 m. p. h. at sea level

KAYDET PT-17; N2S

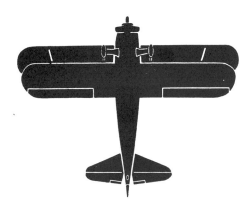

SPAN: 32 ft. 2 in. **SERVICE CEILING:**
LENGTH: 24 ft. 10 in.
MAX. SPEED: 123 m. p. h. at sea level

DISTINGUISHING FEATURES: Single inline engine, low-wing monoplane. Wings have moderate equal taper with rounded tips. Deep, narrow nose and two open cockpits. High tapered fin and rounded rudder. Tapered tailplane with rounded tips and cut-out. Fixed, unfaired landing gear.

INTEREST: This rugged primary trainer is powered with a Ranger six-cylinder inline air-cooled engine. It has a conventional metal fuselage and plywood covered wings built up of wood spars and ribs. This trainer is stable and is smooth and quick on the controls. The Cornell will forgive many mistakes. It has sometimes been referred to as the "cradle" of the Air Force. A modification of this plane equipped with a radial engine is designated as PT–23 and called the "Recruit."

DISTINGUISHING FEATURES: Single uncowled radial engine biplane. Straight staggered wings with rounded tips and N-shaped struts. Two-place open cockpit. Wide bell-shaped fin and rudder. Fin tapers forward. Tapered tailplane with V cut-out and round tips. Fixed landing gear struts set forward of lower wing.

INTEREST: Many a flying cadet left the ground for the first time in a PT–17 Kaydet primary trainer. It was once described by a well-known general of Army Air Forces as "the most efficient airplane of them all." Like its big brother, the famous B–17 Fortress, the Boeing PT–17 Kaydet has built a widespread reputation for stability and ruggedness. During the 3 years of production not a single plane has been lost in flight testing. Designated as the N2S–3 by the U. S. Navy, the Kaydet has trained more fighting pilots than any other type of primary trainer.

CORNELL PT-19

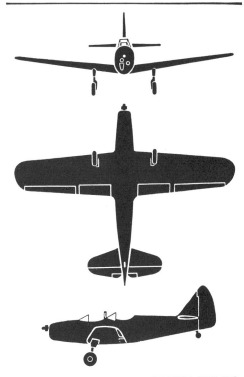

SPAN: 35 ft, 11 in. **SERVICE CEILING:**
LENGTH: 27 ft, 8 in.
MAX. SPEED: 175 m, p. h. at sea level

NAVY: SBD-3, 4, 5
SBD series
ARMY: A-24, A, B

DIVE BOMBER

U.S.A.

SBD "DAUNTLESS"

TAPERING FUSELAGE

DIHEDRAL BREAK

DOUGLAS U.S.A.

PROMINENT UNDERCURVE

SCALE
6-FOOT MAN

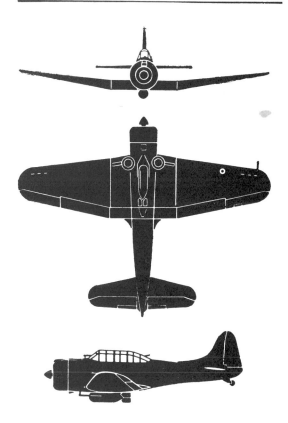

DISTINGUISHING FEATURES: Low-wing monoplane with single radial engine. Wings with equally tapered leading and trailing edges, rounded tips, and dihedral on outer panels. Trailing edge of wing fairs gracefully into tapering fuselage. High single fin and rudder faired forward into fuselage.

INTEREST: This excellent dive bomber is one of the longest lived of all combat aircraft. It has seen much action from carriers of the U. S. Navy in the Pacific, notably in the Coral Sea Battle and at Midway. Long considered to be the finest carrier-based dive bomber in the world, it is now excelled in some respects by the more recently developed Helldiver. As the A–24, the Dauntless is the first dive bomber to be used in quantity by the U. S. Army in support of ground troops. A 1,000-pound bomb is carried in a cradle under center section. Bomb racks are also fitted under the wing roots.

APRIL 1943
FROM DATA CURRENTLY AVAILABLE

WAR DEPARTMENT FM 30–30
NAVY DEPARTMENT BUAER 3

SPAN: 41 ft. 6 in.
LENGTH: 33 ft.
APPROX. MAX. SPEED. 245 m. p. h.

SERVICE CEILING: 25,000 ft.

RESTRICTED

NAVY: **PV-1**
PV-1.3

R.A.F.: VENTURA I, II, III

ARMY. B-34 (B-37)

MEDIUM BOMBER

U.S.A.   U.K.

PV "VENTURA"

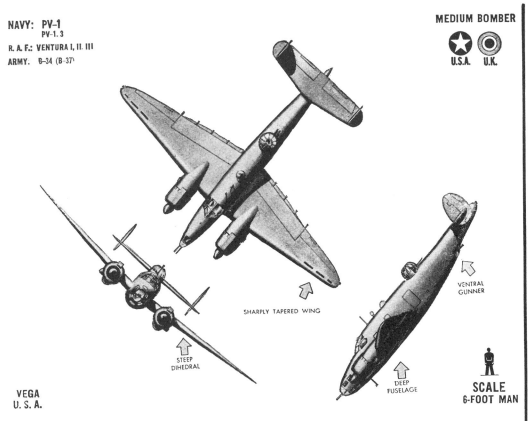

SHARPLY TAPERED WING

STEEP
DIHEDRAL

VENTRAL
GUNNER

DEEP
FUSELAGE

VEGA
U. S. A.

SCALE
6-FOOT MAN

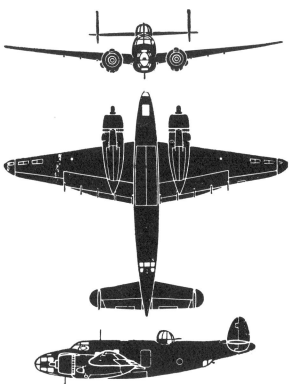

DISTINGUISHING FEATURES: Mid-wing monoplane. Both edges of wing have marked taper. Fowler flap guides are visible. Radial motors are underslung in long nacelles. The fuselage is heavy with a power turret aft of trailing edge of wings. Bottom line of fuselage is broken to accommodate rear guns. Twin fins and rudders are egg-shaped, mounted high and inboard.

INTEREST: The "Ventura" was developed from the Hudson (A-29), which it closely resembles in size and appearance. It has much more powerful engines, however. The prototype of the PV-1 first flew in 1941 and operational models were first reported in action during December 1942 in raids over Holland and Germany. The Army version (B-34) of this aircraft is now in use, along with the A-29, by the R. A. F. Coastal Command for general reconnaissance and other duties.

SPAN: 65 ft. 6 in.
LENGTH: 51 ft. 5 in.
APPROX. MAX. SPEED: over 300 m. p. h.

SERVICE CEILING:
over 32,000 ft.

APRIL 1943
FROM DATA CURRENTLY AVAILABLE

WAR DEPARTMENT FM 30-30
NAVY DEPARTMENT BUAER 3

RESTRICTED

NAVY: F6F-3
F.A.A.: GANNET I

FIGHTER

U.S.A. **U.K.**

F6F "HELLCAT"

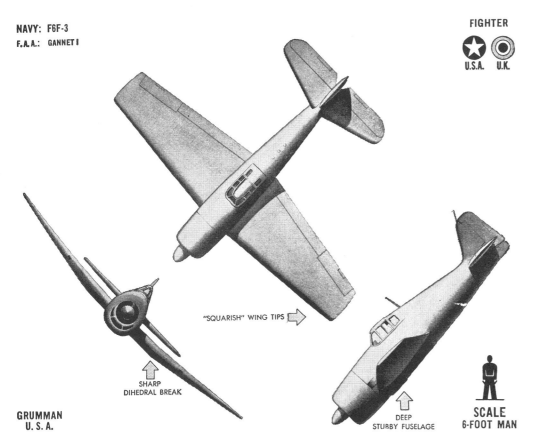

"SQUARISH" WING TIPS ➡

SHARP
DIHEDRAL BREAK ⬆

GRUMMAN
U.S.A.

DEEP
STUBBY FUSELAGE ⬆

**SCALE
6-FOOT MAN**

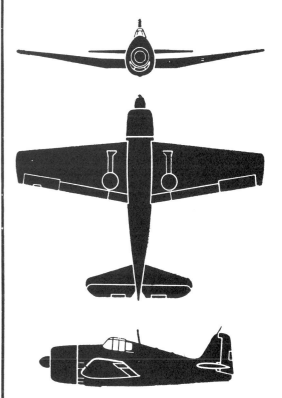

DISTINGUISHING FEATURES: Radial engine, low mid-wing monoplane. Large propeller spinner above center of cowling. Inboard panel of wing horizontal; outboard panels are dihedral. Deep egg-shaped fuselage. High narrow cockpit with straight line running down to tail. Fin and rudder have bluntly rounded top and steep leading and trailing edges. Wing has equally tapered leading and trailing edges and blunt tips. Stabilizer and elevator are long with tapered leading edge, straight trailing edge, and rounded tips.
INTEREST: This new Navy fighter is a carrier-based airplane designed by the Grumman Co. as a successor to the F4F-4. Its performance is similar in many respects to that of the Navy's F4U "Corsair."

APRIL 1943
FROM DATA CURRENTLY AVAILABLE

WAR DEPARTMENT FM 30-30
NAVY DEPARTMENT BUAER 3

SPAN: 42 ft. 10 in.
LENGTH: 33 ft. 6¼ in.
APPROX. MAX. SPEED:

SERVICE CEILING:

NAVY: F4F-3, 4
F4F series: FM-1

F.A.A.: MARTLET I, II

FIGHTER

U.S.A.   U.K.

F4F "WILDCAT"

SQUARE TAIL GROUP

SQUARE WING TIPS

DEEP FIN CURVE
AND HIGH COMBING

DEEP BODIED FUSELAGE
HIGH HUMPED BACK

**SCALE
6-FOOT MAN**

**GRUMMAN
U.S.A.**

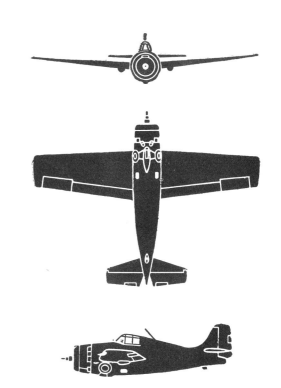

DISTINGUISHING FEATURES: Radial engine mid-wing monoplane. Dihedral from wing roots. Raised cockpit enclosure with straight line running down to the tail. Wings have medium, equal taper with square tips. Fin and rudder have a square top and rather straight trailing edge. Tail tip has an unfinished appearance due to the arrester hook it houses.

INTEREST: This fighter, called the "Martlet" by the British, can be based either on carriers or on land. It is an excellent aircraft and was probably the best carrier-based fighter in battle service until the coming of the newer, heavier, and faster Corsair which is now gradually replacing it. The Wildcat has shown altitude performance approaching that of the Zero. This aircraft was used by the Marines on Wake Island. Lt. Commander O'Hare was flying one when he shot down five Jap aircraft during a single operation.

SPAN: 38 ft.
LENGTH: 28 ft. 11 in.
APPROX. MAX. SPEED: over 310 m. p. h.

SERVICE CEILING:
about 33,000 ft.

RESTRICTED

NAVY: F4U-1
F3A-1; FG-1

F. A. A.: CORSAIR I

FIGHTER

U.S.A. U.K.

F4U "CORSAIR"

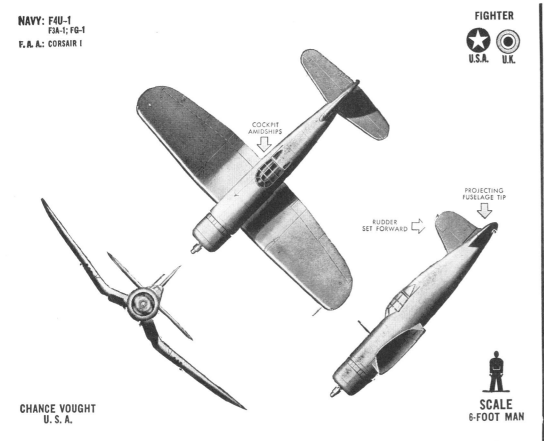

COCKPIT AMIDSHIPS

PROJECTING FUSELAGE TIP

RUDDER SET FORWARD

CHANCE VOUGHT
U. S. A.

SCALE
6-FOOT MAN

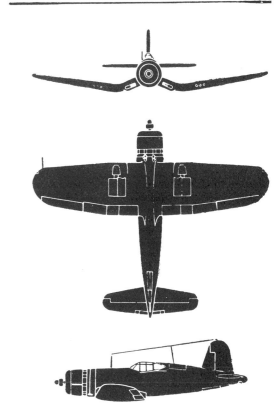

DISTINGUISHING FEATURES: Single radial engine low-wing monoplane. Inverted gull wing. Outer section of the wing is slightly tapered with rounded tips. Nose is medium length and blunt. Fuselage is round with a small cockpit enclosure. The single fin-and-rudder is equally tapered and is rounded on top and set forward of elevators.

INTEREST: This is one of the fastest ship-borne fighters in operation today. The large inverted gull wing was designed to give added clearance for the long propeller blades which are required to absorb the output of the F4U's 2000 h. p. engine. The lower wing position due to the gull design also increases the air cushion effect between deck and plane during landing.

SPAN: 41 ft.
LENGTH: 33 ft. 4 in.
APPROX. MAX. SPEED: 365 m. p. h.

SERVICE CEILING:
over 34,000 ft.

APRIL 1943
FROM DATA CURRENTLY AVAILABLE

WAR DEPARTMENT FM 30—30
NAVY DEPARTMENT BUAER 3

RESTRICTED

NAVY: SB2C–1, 2
   SBW–1; SBF–1

ARMY: A–25, A

F.A.A.:}} HELLDIVER
R.A.F.:

DIVE BOMBER

U.S.A.   U.K.

SB2C "HELLDIVER"

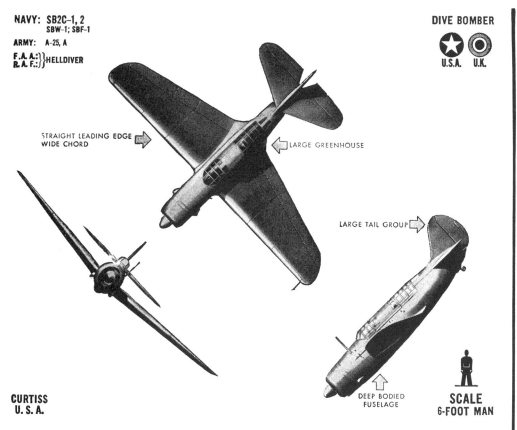

STRAIGHT LEADING EDGE
WIDE CHORD →

← LARGE GREENHOUSE

LARGE TAIL GROUP ▷

↑ DEEP BODIED
FUSELAGE

SCALE
6-FOOT MAN

**CURTISS
U. S. A.**

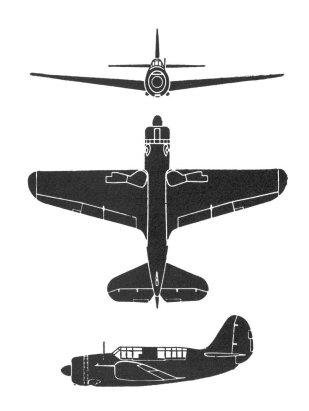

DISTINGUISHING FEATURES: Single radial engine low mid-wing monóplane. Wings have full dihedral. The leading edge is straight with a sharply tapered trailing edge fairing into fuselage. Large blunt nose with large spinner. Long cockpit enclosure extends aft nearly to high broad fin and rudder. The fin has pronounced taper. Large rounded rudder. The tail plane is mounted high with a V cut-out between the elevators.

INTEREST: One of the largest operational single engine aircraft, the Helldiver was designed to carry torpedoes, depth charges, or large bombs.   It can be operated either from carriers or from land bases.   It is faster, and probably carries larger bomb loads than the German "Stuka" Some models of this aircraft will appear with twin floats. From all indications, the SB2C will become one of the world's deadliest dive bombers.

APRIL 1943
FROM DATA CURRENTLY AVAILABLE

WAR DEPARTMENT FM 30–30
NAVY DEPARTMENT BUAER 3

SPAN: 49 ft. 9 in.
LENGTH: 36 ft. 8 in.
APPROX. MAX. SPEED: over 300 m. p. h.

SERVICE CEILING:
over 25,000 ft.

RESTRICTED

NAVY: TBF-1

F.A.A.: TARPON I

TORPEDO BOMBER

U.S.A. U.K.

TBF "AVENGER"

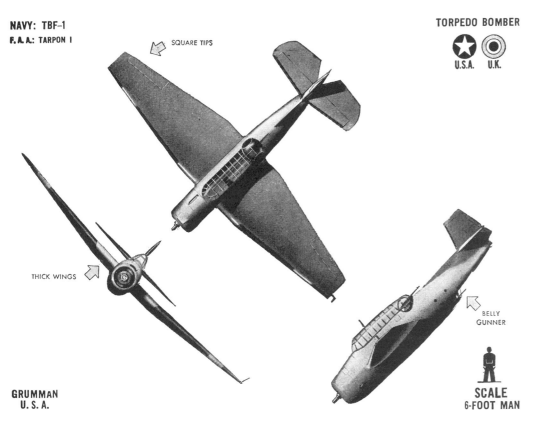

SQUARE TIPS

THICK WINGS

BELLY GUNNER

SCALE
6-FOOT MAN

GRUMMAN
U. S. A.

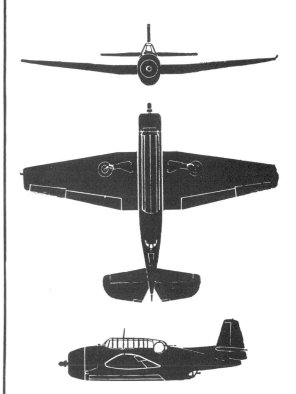

DISTINGUISHING FEATURES: Mid-wing monoplane with single radial engine. Fuselage is short and heavy with break on underside aft of torpedo housing. Wing has sharp taper in outer panels with square cut tips and dihedral on outer panels. Large cockpit enclosure mounted on top of fuselage with bubble turret aft forming part of it. Stabilizer and elevator are set above fuselage and have taper on both edges with nearly square tips. Fin and rudder are high and angular.

INTEREST: The Avenger is probably the best carrier-based torpedo plane so far seen in action. It first gained wide publicity in the Battle of Midway. Probably the most versatile of all torpedo bombers, the TBF has been used as bomber, scout, and for subpatrol from land bases. The deep fuselage permits it to carry a 21″ torpedo or approximately 2000 pounds of bombs internally.

SPAN: 54 ft. 2 in.
LENGTH: 41 ft.
APPROX. MAX. SPEED: 270 m. p. h.

SERVICE CEILING:
22,000 ft.

RESTRICTED

APRIL 1943
FROM DATA CURRENTLY AVAILABLE

WAR DEPARTMENT FM 30–30
NAVY DEPARTMENT BUAER 3

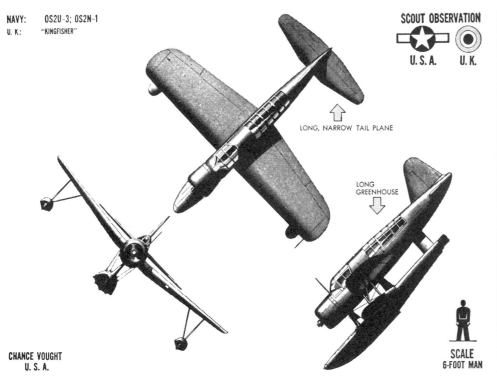

NAVY: OS2U-3; OS2N-1
U. K.: "KINGFISHER"

SCOUT OBSERVATION

U.S.A.   U.K.

LONG, NARROW TAIL PLANE

LONG
GREENHOUSE

SCALE
6-FOOT MAN

CHANCE VOUGHT
U. S. A.

KINGFISHER OS2U (Seaplane)

DISTINGUISHING FEATURES: Low mid-wing monoplane with single float. Wing has straight leading edge, slightly tapered trailing edge and curved tips. Long faired greenhouse extending nearly to the tail. Narrow, diamond-shaped tailplane with round tips set aft of the fin. Tapered fin and rudder with round tip. Single float supported by two faired struts beneath the wing and a wide plate strut at the after end. Prominent wing-tip floats.

INTEREST: The principal function of the Kingfisher is to spot gunfire for the Fleet. It is designed for catapulting from battleships or cruisers and has replaced the Curtiss SOC as the principal observation floatplane of the U. S. Navy.

SPAN: 35 ft. 11 in.   **SERVICE CEILING:**
LENGTH: 33 ft. 10 in.   13,000
MAX. SPEED: 164 m. p. h. at 5,500 ft.

NAVY: SO3C-2
SO3C-1, 2, 3, 4
SOR-1

F.A.A.: SEAMEW I

RECONNAISSANCE

U.S.A.   U.K.

S03C "SEAGULL"

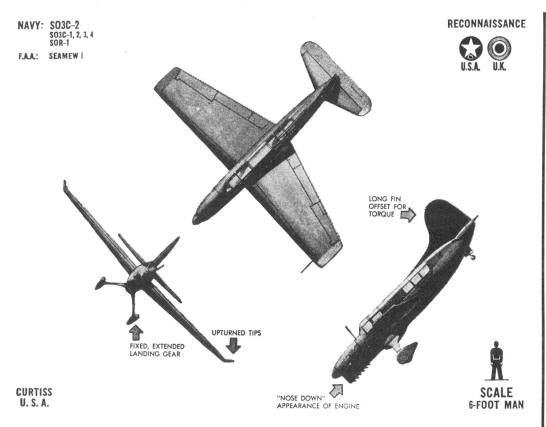

LONG FIN OFFSET FOR TORQUE

UPTURNED TIPS

FIXED, EXTENDED LANDING GEAR

CURTISS
U. S. A.

"NOSE DOWN" APPEARANCE OF ENGINE

SCALE
6-FOOT MAN

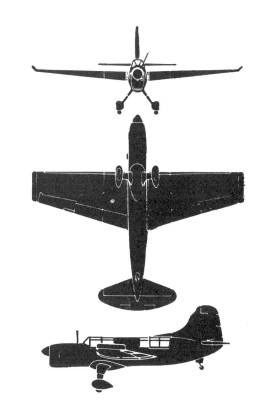

DISTINGUISHING FEATURES: Single-engine mid-wing monoplane. Fixed landing gear or single large float with fixed wing floats. In-line engine and large spinner. Slightly dihedral wings which have straight leading edge and tapered trailing edge. Wing tips square and turned up. Long high cockpit enclosure. Large fin and rudder.

INTEREST: One of the newest battleship and cruiser based airplanes in service, the Seagull is designed for operation as gun spotter for the fleet. It can also be used for anti-submarine patrol on the coast. An interesting feature of the Seagull is that it is powered by an in-line engine which is air-cooled. Equipped for catapult launching, the Seagull can be easily landed in rough waters and is known for its long range. Some versions with fixed landing gear, can be used on carriers. Seagulls now being added to the British Fleet Air Arm are to be known as "Seamews."

APRIL 1943
FROM DATA CURRENTLY AVAILABLE

WAR DEPARTMENT FM 30–30
NAVY DEPARTMENT BUAER 3

SPAN: 38 ft.
LENGTH: 34 ft.
APPROX. MAX. SPEED: 180 m. p. h.

SERVICE CEILING: 18,000 ft.

RESTRICTED

NAVY: **PBM-3**
PBM-1, 3, 4

P. A. F: MARINER I

LONG, THIN WING

PATROL BOMBER—TRANSPORT

U.S.A.   U.K.

PBM "MARINER"

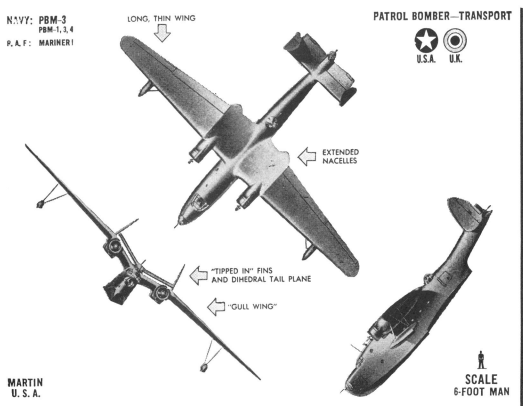

EXTENDED
NACELLES

"TIPPED IN" FINS
AND DIHEDRAL TAIL PLANE

"GULL WING"

**MARTIN
U. S. A.**

SCALE
6-FOOT MAN

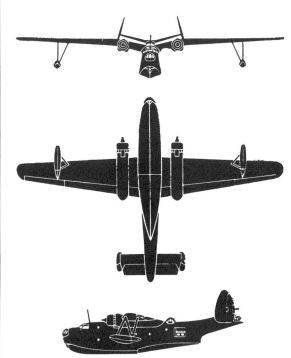

DISTINGUISHING FEATURES: High gull-wing monoplane with twin radial engines. Wings tapered on trailing edge with small rounded tips. Twin toed-in triangular fin and rudders set outboard of dihedral tail plane. Hull tapers back toward tail with sharp step on underside.

INTEREST: The Mariner is an extremely serviceable long-range flying boat. It has been giving excellent results over rough seas and under otherwise strenuous operating conditions. This aircraft was first designed,

built, and flown in miniature. Two torpedoes or equivalent weight in bombs are carried under the wings inboard of the engines. On the PBM-3, fixed wing floats have replaced the retractable floats of the two previous models. At present, some Mariners are being used for over-water transport airplanes. These converted airplanes, with armament removed, will be designated as PBM-3R's. The latest model (not here shown) has 3 power-driven turrets and is called the PBM-3C.

SPAN: 118 ft.
LENGTH: 80 ft.
APPROX. MAX. SPEED: 205 m. p. h.

SERVICE CEILING:
17,000 ft.

RESTRICTED

APRIL 1943
FROM DATA CURRENTLY AVAILABLE

WAR DEPARTMENT FM 30—30
NAVY DEPARTMENT BUAER 3

NAVY: PBY–5
PBY–1, 2, 3, 4, 5
PBN–1, PB2B–1

R. A. F.: CATALINA I, II, III

ARMY: OA–10

RUSSIA: GST

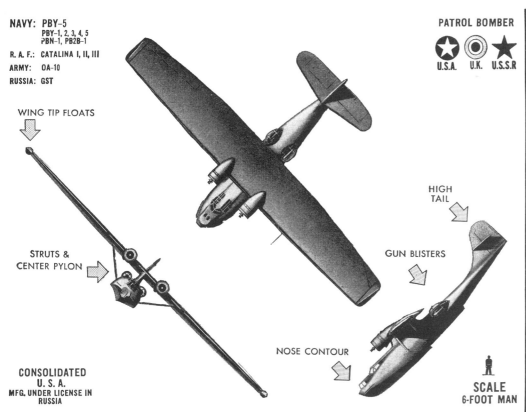

WING TIP FLOATS

STRUTS & CENTER PYLON

CONSOLIDATED U. S. A.
MFG. UNDER LICENSE IN RUSSIA

PATROL BOMBER

★ U.S.A. ◉ U.K. ★ U.S.S.R

HIGH TAIL

GUN BLISTERS

NOSE CONTOUR

SCALE 6-FOOT MAN

PBY "CATALINA"

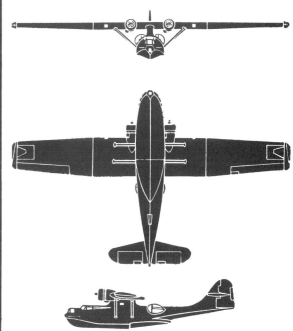

DISTINGUISHING FEATURES: Two-engine parasol-wing monoplane with nearly rectangular wings having square tips. The wing is mounted above the hull on a streamlined superstructure and braced by struts. Wing tip floats are retractable. Two large blister turrets behind wing on hull. Bottom of hull has two steps and sweeps upward to high single fin and rudder.

INTEREST: The "Cat" spotted the German battleship "Bismarck" after the sinking of the British battleship

"Hood." Its capacity to stay long hours in the air makes this aircraft ideally suited for its long sub-spotting and convoy-guarding patrols. In the Aleutians and Solomons, the PBY is reported to have been used as a torpedo bomber, carrying two torpedoes under the wing. Alternatively, it can carry eight 325-lb. depth charges or two 2,000-lb. bombs under the wing. The Catalina is built under license in Russia with some modification in armament and engines. The Russian designation is GST.

SPAN: 104 ft.
LENGTH: 63 ft. 11 in.
APPROX. MAX. SPEED: 170 m. p. h.

SERVICE CEILING
19,000 ft

APRIL 1943
FROM DATA CURRENTLY AVAILABLE

WAR DEPARTMENT FM 30–30
NAVY DEPARTMENT BUAER 3

NAVY: PB2Y-3
PB2Y-2, 3

R. A. F.: CORONADO

U.S.A. U.K.

PB2Y "CORONADO"

WING TIP FLOATS

DIHEDRAL TAIL

SQUARE TIPPED WINGS

SCALE
6-FOOT MAN

CONSOLIDATED
U. S. A.

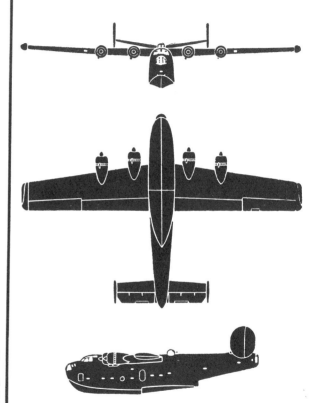

DISTINGUISHING FEATURES: Four-engine high-wing monoplane. Deep hull with prominent steps tapering toward rear. Leading edge of wing is tapered. Trailing edge straight. Square wing tips. Large rounded twin outboard rudders mounted on a dihedral tail plane.
INTEREST: The Coronado is a long-range four-engine seaplane of great size, power, and range. It is used mainly as a patrol bomber but in many instances it has been converted for transport purposes in which case it is called the PB2Y-3R. The transport version has gun positions removed and fuselage faired in. The wing tip floats are retractable. The twin fins and rudders are practically identical with those of the B-24 Liberator which is made by the same company.

SPAN: 115 ft.
LENGTH: 79 ft. 3 in.
APPROX. MAX. SPEED: 219 m. p. h.

SERVICE CEILING:
20,000 ft.

APRIL 1943
FROM DATA CURRENTLY AVAILABLE

WAR DEPARTMENT FM 30—30
NAVY DEPARTMENT BUAER 3

OS2U "KINGFISHER"

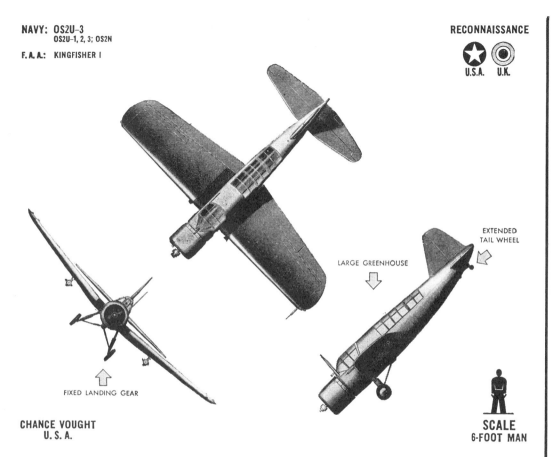

LARGE GREENHOUSE

EXTENDED TAIL WHEEL

FIXED LANDING GEAR

**CHANCE VOUGHT
U. S. A.**

**SCALE
6-FOOT MAN**

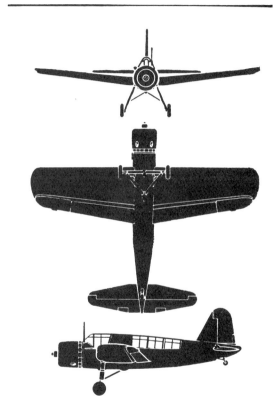

DISTINGUISHING FEATURES: Low mid - wing monoplane with straight leading edge and tapered trailing edge. Long high cockpit enclosure extending nearly to the tail. Bottom line is broken by a fixed landing gear or floats. Tall triangular fin and rudder.

INTEREST: Known as "The eyes of the Navy", the principal function of the Kingfisher is to spot gunfire for the fleet. Some versions are equipped with wheels for scouting operations from land bases. Fitted with a single float, the Kingfisher is designed for catapulting from battleships or cruisers.

SPAN: 36 ft.
LENGTH: 33 ft. 10 in. as seaplane
30 ft. 1 in. as landplane
APPROX. MAX. SPEED: 175 m. p. h.

SERVICE CEILING:
about 12,000 ft.

APRIL 1943
FROM DATA CURRENTLY AVAILABLE

WAR DEPARTMENT FM 30–30
NAVY DEPARTMENT BUAER 3

RESTRICTED

NAVY: SB2A-2
ARMY: A-34
U. K.: BERMUDA

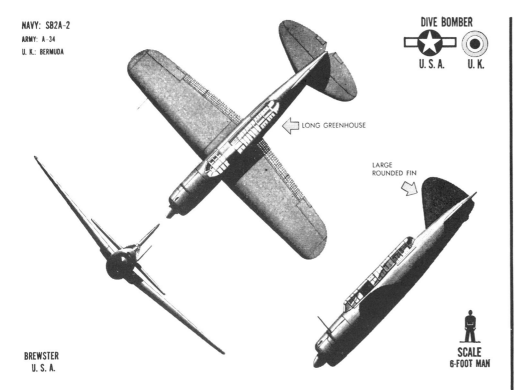

LONG GREENHOUSE

LARGE
ROUNDED FIN

BREWSTER
U. S. A.

DIVE BOMBER

U. S. A. U. K.

SCALE
6-FOOT MAN

BUCCANEER SB2A

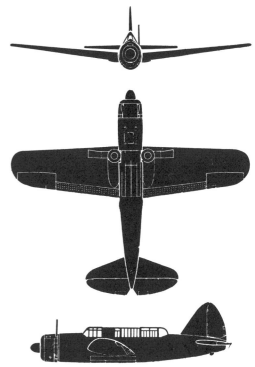

DISTINGUISHING FEATURES: Single radial engine mid-wing monoplane. Wing slightly tapered with more taper on trailing edge and broad rounded tips. Long, oval fuselage with large, unfaired greenhouse extending nearly to the fin. Triangular-shaped fin and rudder has tapered leading edge, curved trailing edge with V cut-out in center and rounded tips.

INTEREST: This Brewster-made dive bomber has been nicknamed the "Bermuda" by the British. Although this plane has not been used extensively in actual combat, it is used by both the U. S. Navy and the British Fleet Air Arm as an advanced dive-bomber trainer.

SPAN: 47 ft.
LENGTH: 39 ft. 2 in.
MAX. SPEED: 274 m. p. h. at 12,000 ft.
SERVICE CEILING: 24,900 ft.

RESTRICTED

NAVY: SO3C-1
F. A. A. SEAMEW

SCOUT OBSERVATION

U. S. A.

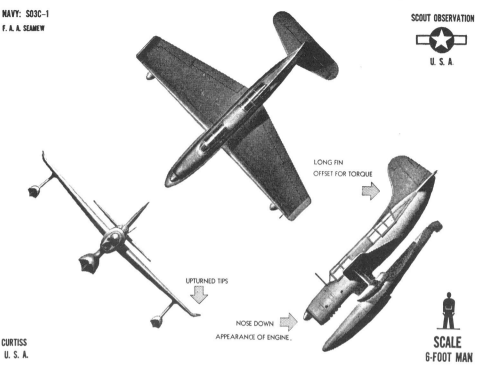

LONG FIN
OFFSET FOR TORQUE

UPTURNED TIPS

NOSE DOWN
APPEARANCE OF ENGINE.

SCALE
6-FOOT MAN

CURTISS
U. S. A.

SEAGULL SO3C (Seaplane)

DISTINGUISHING FEATURES: Single-engine, mid-wing monoplane. Single large float with fixed wing floats. Wing has straight leading edge, tapered trailing edge, and square upturned tips. Fuselage narrow with long greenhouse faired back to the tail. Deep inline engine has a nose-down appearance with spinner at top. Large rounded fin and rudder sweeps forward over rear of greenhouse. Tailplane set back with straight trailing edge, tapered leading edge and round tips.

INTEREST: The Seagull is designed for operation as gun spotter for the Fleet. An interesting feature is the air-cooled, inverted, inline engine. Equipped for catapult launching, the Seagull can be easily landed in rough waters and is known for its long range. This plane is known as the "Seamew" in the British Fleet Air Arm. Some of the earlier Seagulls have a curved trailing edge on the elevator.

SPAN: 38 ft.
LENGTH: 35 ft.
MAX. SPEED: 183 m. p. h. at 12,000 ft.

SERVICE CEILING:
15,200 ft.

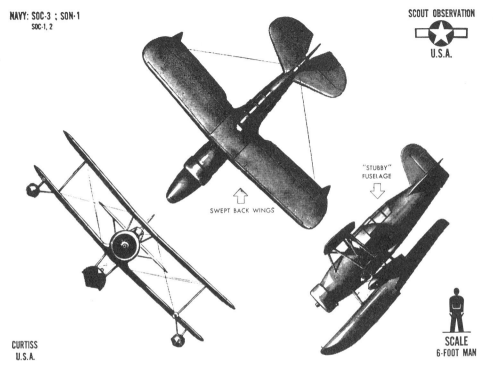

NAVY: SOC-3 ; SON-1
SOC-1, 2

SCOUT OBSERVATION
U.S.A.

SWEPT BACK WINGS

"STUBBY" FUSELAGE

SCALE
6-FOOT MAN

CURTISS
U.S.A.

DISTINGUISHING FEATURES: Single radial engine biplane with large single float. Equal-span rectangular wings have rounded tips and are slightly swept back and staggered. N-shaped struts and small wing-tip floats. Short deep fuselage with large cockpit enclosure faired abruptly at the rear. Large tailplane has tapered leading edge, rounded tips and very large cut-out in trailing edge. Single fin and rudder has vertical trailing edge, tapered leading edge, and rounded tip.

INTEREST: Although obsolete, this plane is still used on many battleships and cruisers for spotting gunfire and for scouting purposes. It is sturdily built for catapult take-offs and landings in rough weather. Its slow speed and ease of handling make it ideally suited for spotting.

NOV. 1943
FROM DATA CURRENTLY AVAILABLE

SUPPLEMENT ONE [WAR DEPARTMENT FM 30—30
NAVY DEPARTMENT BUAER 3

CURTISS SOC (Seaplane)

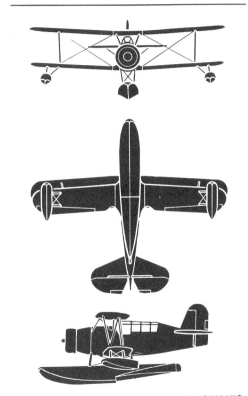

SPAN: 36 ft.
LENGTH: 31 ft. 9 in.
MAX. SPEED: 162 m. p. h. at 800 ft.

SERVICE CEILING: 13,300 ft.

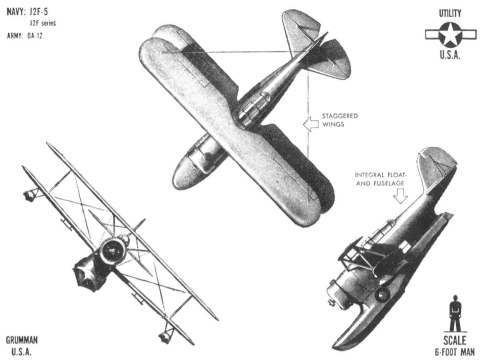

UTILITY

U.S.A.

STAGGERED
WINGS

INTEGRAL FLOAT
AND FUSELAGE

SCALE
6-FOOT MAN

GRUMMAN
U.S.A.

DUCK J2F

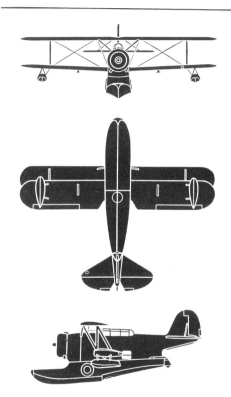

DISTINGUISHING FEATURES: Single radial engine biplane. Large single float faired into underside of fuselage giving a heavy squat appearance. Straight, staggered, equal-span wings have rounded tips. **N**-strut bracing and small fixed wing-tip floats. Unfaired cockpit enclosure. Round, tapered fin and rudder. Horizontal tailplane sharply tapered on leading edge with small curved tips, curved trailing edge and cut-out in center.

INTEREST: This odd-looking amphibian float-plane has been a standard utility plane in the Navy since 1937. It is used aboard battleships and cruisers as a "Command" plane and can also be used for photographic work.

SPAN: 39 ft.
LENGTH: 34 ft.
MAX. SPEED: 176 m. p. h. at 3,200 ft.

SERVICE CEILING:
18,900 ft.

NAVY: SNJ-3, 4, 5
ARMY: AT-6A
U. K.: HARVARD 1, 11

ADVANCED TRAINER

U.S.A.   U.K.

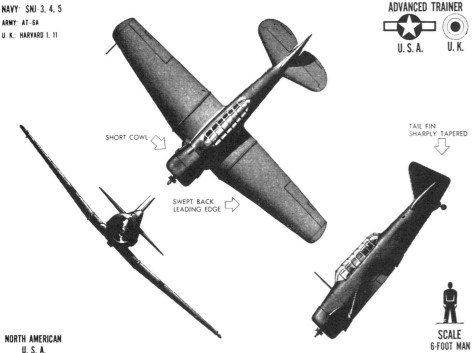

SHORT COWL

SWEPT BACK
LEADING EDGE

TAIL FIN
SHARPLY TAPERED

SCALE
6-FOOT MAN

TEXAN SNJ; AT-6A

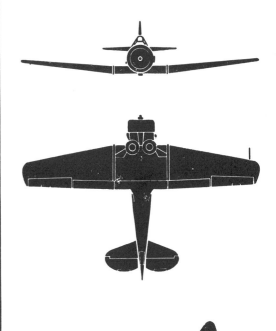

SPAN: 42 ft.   **SERVICE CEILING:**
LENGTH: 29 ft.
MAX. SPEED: 210 m. p. h. at 5,000 ft.

RESTRICTED

NORTH AMERICAN
U. S. A.

DISTINGUISHING FEATURES: Single radial engine, low-wing monoplane. The outer section of the wing has marked dihedral with pronounced taper on the leading edge. The center section is rectangular. Squarish wing tips. Large round nose. Large unfaired cockpit canopy extending beyond trailing edge of wing. High triangular fin and rudder. Tailplane tapers forward and has elliptical-shaped elevators with **V** cut-out.

INTEREST: Now known as the Texan (formerly the Harvard), this advanced trainer has played a vital role in the final stages of pilot training. It is noted for its sturdiness and ease of maintenance. The Texan is powered with a 550-hp. Pratt & Whitney radial engine, and has a weight of approximately 5,200 pounds. It is used as an advanced fighter trainer by nearly all of the United Nations. This plane with a few minor modifications is manufactured under license in Australia, where it is known as the Whirraway. The Whirraway has been used on occasion as a dive bomber

R. A. F.: BEAUFIGHTER I
BEAUFIGHTER I, II, VI

"BEAUFIGHTER"

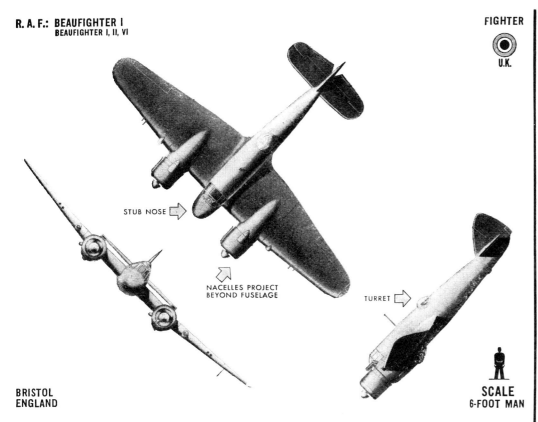

STUB NOSE ➡

NACELLES PROJECT
BEYOND FUSELAGE ➡

TURRET ➡

**BRISTOL
ENGLAND**

**SCALE
6-FOOT MAN**

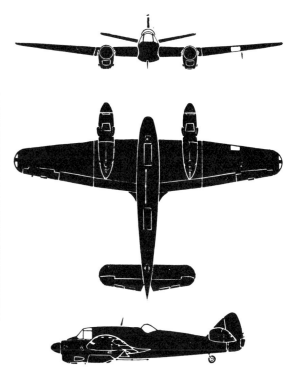

DISTINGUISHING FEATURES: Twin engine, mid-wing monoplane. Wing has equal taper in outer sections with wide flat center section and rounded tips. The twin radial engines protrude beyond the very short stubby nose. Fin and rudder are of the broad triangular Bristol type. Tail plane has marked dihedral with slight taper on trailing edge and V cut-out.
INTEREST: The Beaufighter was developed from the Beaufort bomber to fill the need for a heavily armed twin engine long range fighter. Although used principally as a night fighter, it rivals the Hurricane for versatility, being used also as a day fighter, a "tank buster," and with the British Coastal Command. It is well liked as a fighter and ground strafer in the Middle East. To counteract swing during take-offs, all Beaufighters are now fitted with a dihedral tail plane. The Beaufighter II has in-line instead of radial engines.

SPAN: 57 ft. 10 in.
LENGTH: 40 ft. 11 in.
MAX. SPEED: 323 m. p. h. at 14,400 ft.

SERVICE CEILING:
29,700 ft.

RESTRICTED

R. A. F.: SPITFIRE V
SPITFIRE series

F. A. A.: SEAFIRE

U. S. ARMY

FIGHTER

U.K.   U.S.A.

"SPITFIRE"

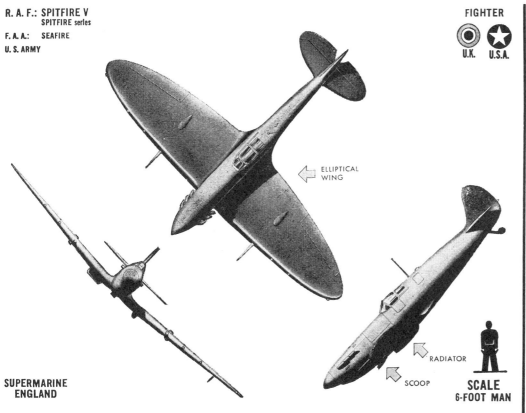

ELLIPTICAL WING

RADIATOR

SCOOP

SCALE
6-FOOT MAN

SUPERMARINE
ENGLAND

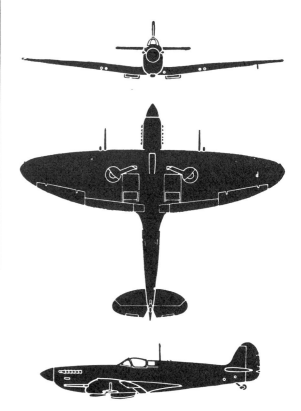

DISTINGUISHING FEATURES: Low-wing monoplane with full dihedral and characteristic elliptically curved wing outline. Radiator intake off-set on underside of wing. Mark IX has radiator intake under both wings. Single in-line engine with large pointed spinner and long narrow fuselage. Stabilizer and elevator are set high on fuselage, with elliptical curved outline and cut-out in trailing edge. The fin and rudder are small and rounded.

INTEREST: The "Spit" played a great part in defeating the Luftwaffe in the Battle of Britain. Its speed, rate of climb, superior maneuverability, and great fire power make it one of the finest single-engine fighters in the world. A carrier-based version, the "Seafire", has been used in the Mediterranean and to protect convoys to Russia. Three latest type "Spits" are reported to have brought down three Ju–86 P pressure cabin aircraft from nearly 50,000 feet in November 1942.

SPAN: 36 ft. 10 in.
LENGTH: 30 ft. 4 in.
MAX. SPEED: 375 m. p. h. at 20,250 ft.

SERVICE CEILING·
37,700 ft.

APRIL 1943
FROM DATA CURRENTLY AVAILABLE

WAR DEPARTMENT FM 30–30
NAVY DEPARTMENT BUAER 3

RESTRICTED

R. A. F., F. A. A.: TYPHOON I

FIGHTER

U.K.

"TYPHOON"

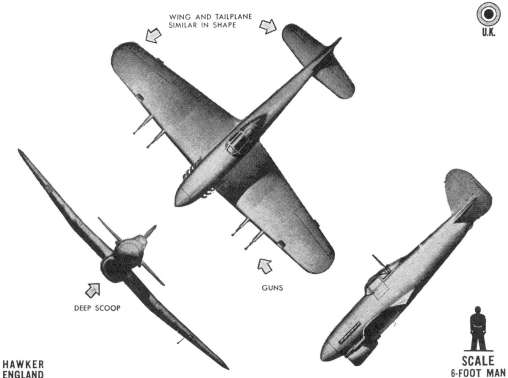

WING AND TAILPLANE
SIMILAR IN SHAPE

GUNS

DEEP SCOOP

**HAWKER
ENGLAND**

SCALE
6-FOOT MAN

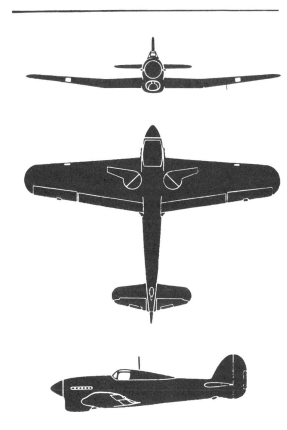

DISTINGUISHING FEATURES: Low-wing monoplane with single in-line engine. Dihedral on outer wing panels only. Short pointed nose. Equally tapered wings with rounded tips. Large radiator intake under nose. Well-curved fin and rudder, extending slightly below fuselage.
INTEREST: The newest member of the famous Hurricane "family" and one of the latest surprises for the enemy. Its designer was drawing plans for this air-craft two years before the outbreak of war. With a speed of over 400 miles per hour, the Typhoon has been built around one of the world's most powerful engines. Its creator showed his vision in that instead of designing his ship and getting an engine, he found his engine and built a ship to fit it. This high-altitude fighter in some respects resembles a Hurricane, but is much larger and from the side views does not have the hump-back appearance of the Hurricane.

SPAN: 41 ft. 7 in.
LENGTH: 31 ft. 8½ in.
MAX. SPEED:

SERVICE CEILING:

RESTRICTED

FIGHTER

U.K.

UNIFORM TAPER

STRAIGHT BACK

STEEP DIHEDRAL

**FAIREY
ENGLAND**

SCOOP

**SCALE
6-FOOT MAN**

FULMAR

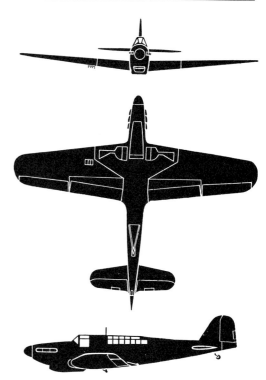

SPAN: 46 ft.   **SERVICE CEILING:**
LENGTH: 40 ft. 4 in.   23,000 ft.
APPROX. SPEED: 250 m. p. h. at 10,000 ft.

RESTRICTED

DISTINGUISHING FEATURES: Low-wing monoplane with single inline engine. Wings are equi-tapered with rounded tips. Fuselage is long and narrow, with long cockpit canopy fairing into fuselage. Airscoop beneath nose. Wide fin and rudder with pronounced taper on leading edge. Tailplane sets low and well forward on the fuselage and is similar in shape to wing.

INTEREST: An eight-gun carrier-based fighter of the British Fleet Air Arm, the Fulmar has a greater range than many land fighters with similar armament. This is an important advantage, since frequent landings on carriers for purposes of refueling are a distinct nuisance. Although this plane is now obsolescent, it has done good work in the Mediterranean in clashes with Italian planes.

R. A. F.: HURRICANE IIc
  HURRICANE I, II
  HURRIBOMBER

F. A. A.: SEA HURRICANE

RUSSIA

FIGHTER—LIGHT BOMBER

U.K.   U.S.S.R.

"HURRICANE"

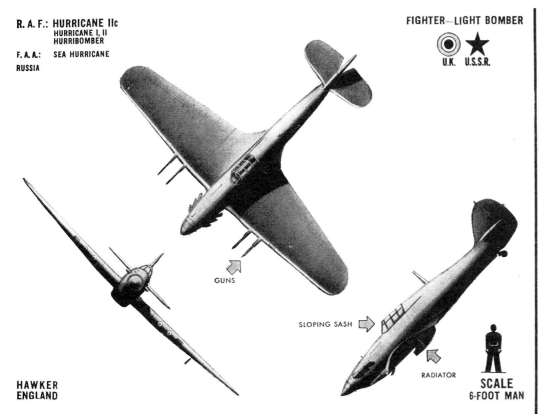

GUNS

SLOPING SASH

RADIATOR

SCALE
6-FOOT MAN

HAWKER
ENGLAND

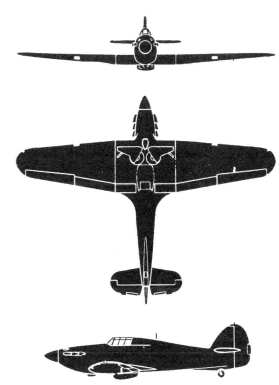

DISTINGUISHING FEATURES: Low-wing monoplane with single in-line engine. Wings have slight dihedral and equal taper in outer section, with rounded tips. Fuselage has hump-back effect and pointed nose, with large air-scoop on underside below cockpit. Very large rounded fin and rudder. Stabilizer and elevator have rounded tips with cut-away in trailing edge.
INTEREST: Hurricanes, along with Spitfires, played an outstanding role in the Battle of Britain. In fact, Hurricanes shot down more aircraft than all other types put together. Although early models were used almost exclusively for interception at high altitudes, more recently this aircraft has been used for low-level bombing, dive bombing, and night fighting. As a carrier-based fighter with the Fleet Air Arm, it has done outstanding work in protecting convoys to Russia. Some versions carry as many as 12 machine guns, while others mount four 20-mm. cannon. For tropical service the Hurricane is equipped with a large scoop under the nose.

SPAN: 40 ft.
LENGTH: 31 ft. 5 in.
APPROX. SPEED: 335 m. p. h. at 22,000 ft.

SERVICE CEILING:
36,600 ft.

RESTRICTED

R. A. F.: MOSQUITO IV
MOSQUITO series

LIGHT BOMBER—FIGHTER

U.K.

"MOSQUITO"

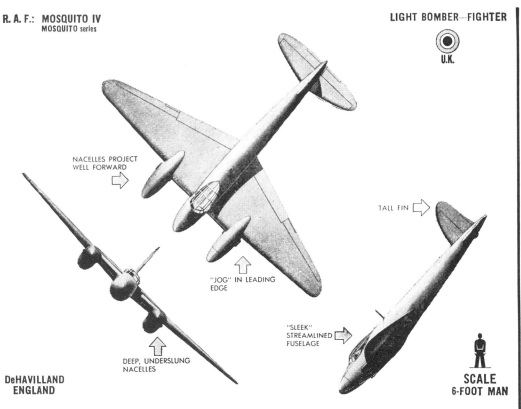

NACELLES PROJECT WELL FORWARD →

TALL FIN →

↑ "JOG" IN LEADING EDGE

← "SLEEK" STREAMLINED FUSELAGE

↑ DEEP, UNDERSLUNG NACELLES

DeHAVILLAND ENGLAND

SCALE 6-FOOT MAN

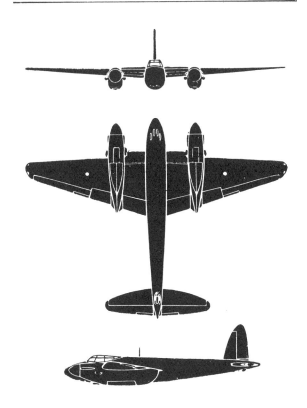

DISTINGUISHING FEATURES: Twin engine, high mid-wing monoplane. Leading edge of wing inboard of engines is farther forward than outer section. Trailing edge of wing has pronounced taper with rounded tips. In-line engines are underslung and protrude forward nearly as far as the short nose. Fuselage is long and narrow with wide raised cockpit forward of wings. Extremely tall single fin and rudder set forward. In certain models the engine nacelles protrude beyond the trailing edge.

INTEREST: This reconnaissance bomber, one of the fastest aircraft of its type, became operational during the latter part of 1942. In raids over Europe it has outdistanced the F. W. 190's sent up to intercept it. It attracted considerable attention when it was used to bomb Berlin on the first daylight raid on that city. A particularly clean aircraft in appearance, the Mosquito is constructed for the most part of plywood. There is also a multi-seat fighter version with nontransparent nose.

SPAN: 54 ft. 2 in.
LENGTH: 40 ft. 9½ in.
MAX. SPEED:

SERVICE CEILING:

RESTRICTED

"BEAUFORT"

TURRET

HIGH GREENHOUSE

**BRISTOL
ENGLAND**

**SCALE
6-FOOT MAN**

DISTINGUISHING FEATURES: Mid-wing monoplane with twin radial engines underslung. Bell shaped fuselage section. Dihedral on outer wing panels. Equitapered wings with rounded tips. Tapered trailing edge to elevator with V cut-out. Mid-turret faired into cabin. Fin and rudder are of the broad Bristol type.

INTEREST: The Beaufort is one of the principal reconnaissance aircraft of the R. A. F. Coastal Command. It is used for torpedo attacks on coastal shipping, for mine laying and for low level bombing of German occupied ports. The success of this aircraft led to the use of its basic design for development of the Beaufighter. For torpedo attacks, the Beaufort is faster than the Albacore torpedo bombers of the British Fleet Air Arm. Not being equipped with dive brakes, it usually uses a low flat approach to keep its speed low enough to launch the torpedo successfully. The newer models do not have the rounded plates projecting beyond the trailing edge of the wing.

APRIL 1943
FROM DATA CURRENTLY AVAILABLE

WAR DEPARTMENT FM 30—30
NAVY DEPARTMENT BUAER 3

SPAN: 57 ft. 10 in.
LENGTH: 44 ft. 2 in.
MAX SPEED: 275 m. p. h. at 6,500 ft.

SERVICE CEILING:
19,000 ft. (overload)

RESTRICTED

R. A. F.: HAMPDEN

LIGHT BOMBER

U.K.

TRIANGULAR WING
TRAILING EDGE SWEPT FORWARD

THICK AND THIN
FORE AND AFT

DEEP, NARROW
FUSELAGE

HANDLEY-PAGE
ENGLAND

SCALE
6-FOOT MAN

"HAMPDEN"

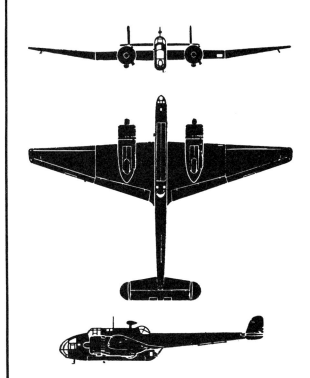

DISTINGUISHING FEATURES: Mid - wing monoplane with two radial engines. Wing has marked taper on trailing edge with small raked tips. Fuselage is extremely long and narrow in plan. In side elevation, the fuselage is deep to trailing edge of wing where there is a sharp step on both top and bottom. Aft of the wing, the fuselage is very small, tapering back to the stabilizer. Twin fins and rudders are set slightly inboard on stabilizer. Stabilizer has slight taper on leading edge. Straight trailing edge and round tips. **INTEREST:** A veteran among twin-engined bombers, the Hampden, although retiring in favor of improved Beauforts and Blenheims, is still doing good work as a mine layer. The Hampden carriers a crew of four.

SPAN: 69 ft. 4 in.
LENGTH: 53 ft. 7 in.
MAX. SPEED: 247 m. p. h. at 13,800 ft.

SERVICE CEILING:
19,000 ft. (max. load)

APRIL 1943
FROM DATA CURRENTLY AVAILABLE

WAR DEPARTMENT FM 30—30
NAVY DEPARTMENT BUAER 3

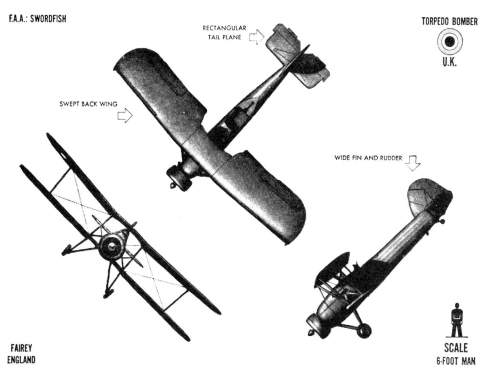

RECTANGULAR TAIL PLANE

SWEPT BACK WING

WIDE FIN AND RUDDER

TORPEDO BOMBER

U.K.

FAIREY
ENGLAND

SCALE
6-FOOT MAN

DISTINGUISHING FEATURES: Single radial engine biplane. Wings have a slight stagger. Bottom wing is shorter and has no dihedral. Top wing has a swept-back appearance with large cut-out in the center. Prominent ring cowling. Semi-circular fin and rudder. Strut-braced tailplane has elevator with large cut-out in center. Elevator extends beyond horizontal stabilizer. Stabilizer has straight leading edge.

INTEREST: The Fairey Swordfish is used by the British Fleet Air Arm for torpedo, spotter, and reconnaissance work. It is sometimes used with twin floats for catapult operations from cruisers and battleships. The carrier version with fixed landing gear is used more extensively. It has a fixed gun firing forward. Older models of this plane have open cockpits for the pilot, observer, and gunner behind the wings. Recent models, however, have a large enclosed cockpit.

SWORDFISH

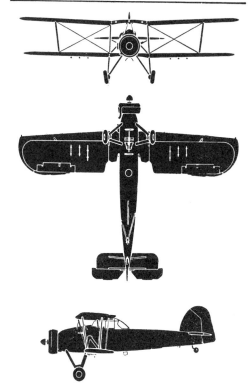

SPAN: 45 ft. 6 in.
LENGTH: 36 ft. 4 in.
MAX. SPEED: 144 m. p. h. at 5,500 ft.

SERVICE CEILING:
17,000 ft.

RESTRICTED

F.A.A.: ALBACORE

TORPEDO BOMBER

U.K.

"ALBACORE"

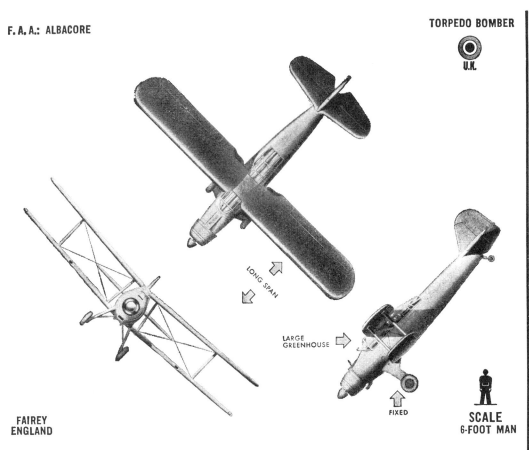

LONG SPAN

LARGE
GREENHOUSE

FIXED

SCALE
6-FOOT MAN

FAIREY
ENGLAND

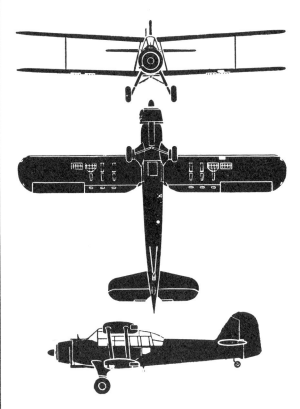

DISTINGUISHING FEATURES: Single bay bi-plane with radial engine. Straight, round tipped wings of equal span. Fixed landing gear. Long high greenhouse. Large single fin and rudder with rounded top.

INTEREST: Nicknamed by the British "The Applecore," this three-place aircraft was designed for operation from carriers or, on floats, from cruisers. Relatively slow and maneuverable, it is well adapted to the diving approach used by the British Fleet Air Arm in daylight torpedo attacks. Developed from the "Swordfish" it is being used to replace that torpedo bomber until modern torpedo carrying aircraft, now being developed, come into use. Compared to most present day torpedo bombers, the Albacore is an obsolete aircraft.

SPAN: 50 ft.
LENGTH: 40 ft.
MAX. SPEED: 172 m. p. h. at 4,800 ft.

SERVICE CEILING:
18,000 ft.

RESTRICTED

R. A. F.: SUNDERLAND I, II

"SUNDERLAND"

ENGINES
TOE OUT ➡

TALL FIN ➡

FIXED FLOATS ➡

DEEP HULL ⬆

**SCALE
6-FOOT MAN**

**SHORT
ENGLAND**

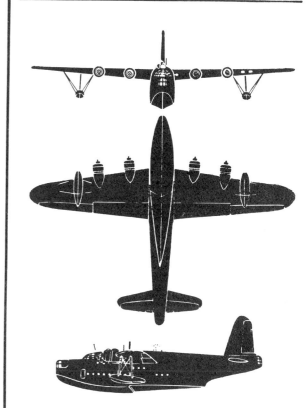

DISTINGUISHING FEATURES: High-wing four-engined monoplane. Very slight dihedral to a thick tapered wing. Deep hull with **V** bottom and rounded top. Two steps lead up to narrow tail, housing a gun position. Four radial engines have small nacelles. Stabilizer and elevator similar in shape to wing. Tall fin and rudder with leading edge tapered.

INTEREST: This large aircraft has performed many and varied duties. One of its tasks is to patrol the ice far

North of the Arctic Circle, reporting movement of the icebergs. It was used in the evacuation of Greece and Crete. These flying boats have cruised far out over the Atlantic protecting convoys to Britain. The Sunderland has shown qualities of reliability and endurance equal to the importance of its duties. A Sunderland forced down in the South Atlantic was towed hundreds of miles by a naval corvette through very stormy weather.

APRIL 1943
FROM DATA CURRENTLY AVAILABLE

WAR DEPARTMENT FM 30–30
NAVY DEPARTMENT BUAER 3

SPAN: 112 ft. 9½ in.
LENGTH: 85 ft. 4 in.
MAX. SPEED: 204 m. p. h. at 5,000 ft.

SERVICE CEILING:
14,100 ft.

F. A. A.: BARRACUDA

RECONNAISSANCE

U.K.

"BARRACUDA"

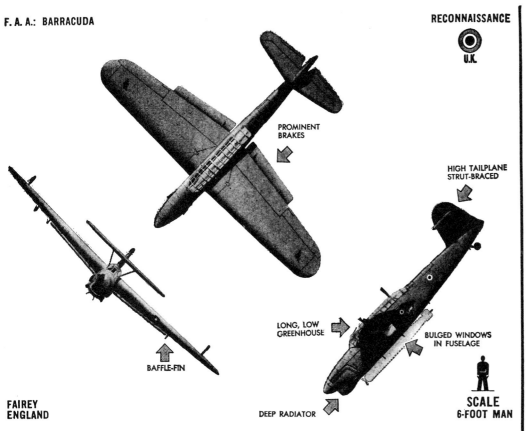

PROMINENT BRAKES

HIGH TAILPLANE STRUT-BRACED

LONG, LOW GREENHOUSE

BULGED WINDOWS IN FUSELAGE

BAFFLE-FIN

FAIREY ENGLAND

DEEP RADIATOR

SCALE 6-FOOT MAN

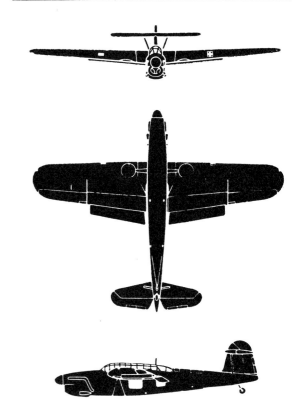

DISTINGUISHING FEATURES: Single in-line engine, high-wing monoplane. Wings have slight dihedral and taper with large rounded tips. Prominent flaps project beyond trailing edge of wings. Narrow diamond-shaped stabilizer and elevator with rounded tips is set high, being mounted on upper part of fin and rudder. Stabilizer is externally braced. Large radiator directly under medium-sized spinner. Fuselage tapers back gradually and has a long sloping cockpit enclosure commencing at leading edge and extending aft of trailing edge of wing. High fin and rudder with rounded top.

INTEREST: This new aircraft is powered with a Rolls Royce Merlin engine. One modification of this plane is in service with fixed landing gear.

SPAN: 49 ft. 2 in.
LENGTH: 40 ft. 7 in.
MAX. SPEED:

SERVICE CEILING:

RESTRICTED

APRIL 1943
FROM DATA CURRENTLY AVAILABLE

WAR DEPARTMENT FM 30—30
NAVY DEPARTMENT BUAER 3

R. A. F.: WELLINGTON IV
WELLINGTON series

MEDIUM BOMBER

U.K.

"WELLINGTON"

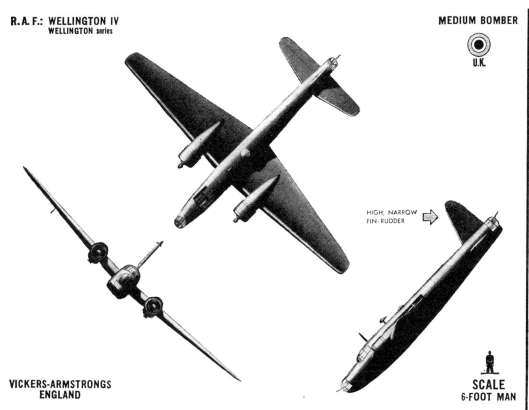

HIGH, NARROW
FIN-RUDDER →

SCALE
6-FOOT MAN

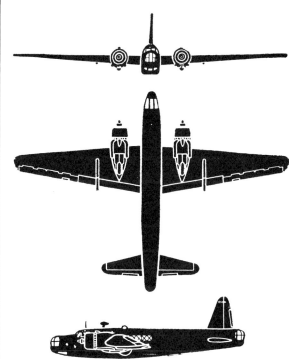

VICKERS-ARMSTRONGS
ENGLAND

DISTINGUISHING FEATURES: Twin engined, mid-wing monoplane. Wellington II has in-line engines; Wellington III, radial engines. Slight dihedral from root of wings. Wings tapered on both edges with raked tips. Deep, heavy fuselage with blunt nose and bulbous tail turret. High triangular fin-and-rudder set in from tail turret. Tail-plane tapered on leading edge with round tips.

INTEREST: The Wellington is one of the most used British bombers. Although heavier and larger aircraft are now being produced, Wellingtons are still constructed in great numbers. Numerous versions, with varying fuselage lengths, have been brought out since the war began. Its geodetic construction (metal basket-weave type of framework) make Wellingtons hard to shoot down. They have often returned safely to their bases with enormous holes in wings or fuselage.

SPAN: 86 ft. 2 in.
LENGTH: 61 ft. (II)
      61 ft. 6 in. (III)
APPROX. MAX. SPEED: 244 m. p. h. at 17,000 ft. (II)

SERVICE CEILING:
(II) 18,000 ft. (overload)

APRIL 1943
FROM DATA CURRENTLY AVAILABLE

WAR DEPARTMENT FM 30-30
NAVY DEPARTMENT BUAER 3

RESTRICTED

"BLENHEIM"

THICK WING

LARGE
RADIAL ENGINES

STRAIGHT BACK

SCALE
6-FOOT MAN

BRISTOL
ENGLAND

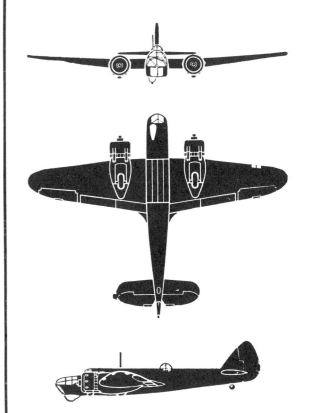

DISTINGUISHING FEATURES: Mid-wing monoplane with twin radial engines. Dihedral on outer wing panels. Equally tapered wing with elliptically curved tips. Cutaway in trailing edge of typical Bristol stabilizer and elevator. Partly retractable dorsal turret and high pointed fin and rudder.

INTEREST: The Blenheim was a standby of the R. A. F. in the early part of the war when it performed admirably as a bomber and as a long-range fighter over France and Norway. After the Norwegian campaign, not much was heard of the Blenheim until it was used in the North African campaigns and in the Middle East. The most recent version, the Mark V, is chiefly adapted for close support work with ground troops. One interesting feature of some Blenheims is the offset blister under the nose containing a rear firing gun which the navigator, who faces forward, controls by a system of mirrors. The Blenheim I has a much shorter nose, the fuselage length being 39 ft. 9 in.

SPAN: 56 ft.
LENGTH: 42 ft. 7 in.
MAX. SPEED: 260 m. p. h. at 12,000 ft.

SERVICE CEILING:
26,500 ft.

RESTRICTED

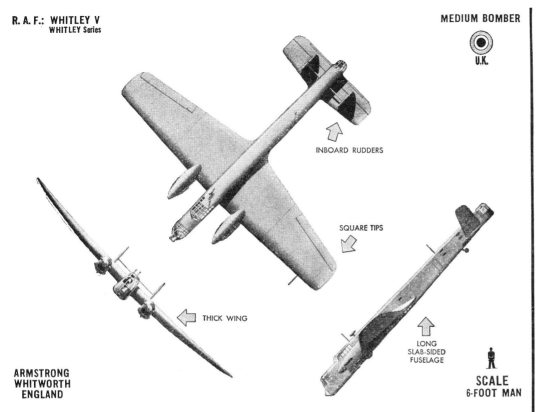

INBOARD RUDDERS

SQUARE TIPS

THICK WING

LONG SLAB-SIDED FUSELAGE

SCALE
6-FOOT MAN

ARMSTRONG
WHITWORTH
ENGLAND

DISTINGUISHING FEATURES: Mid - wing monoplane with twin in-line engines close to fuselage. Wings have marked taper on trailing edge with rounded, blunt tips. Fuselage is long and narrow, tapering upward in a straight line from nose to tail. Dihedral in outboard panels only. Blunt nose with under-slung appearance. Engines underslung. Nearly rectangular stabilizer and elevator set very low with twin fins and rudders set atop and well inboard. Large tail gun position.

INTEREST: The first British bombs of the present war to fall on the soil of the German mainland were dropped on the night of May 11, 1940, when a force of 18 Whitley bombers attacked railroad communications behind the lines of the German advance across the low countries. The latest Whitleys, the Mark V's, are still in operation with the British Coastal Command doing anti-submarine duty and minelaying. The Whitley I, II, and III, now obsolescent, have radial engines and wider fins with curved leading edge.

SPAN: 84 ft
LENGTH: 72 ft. 6 in.
MAX. SPEED: 221 m. p. h. at 17,750 ft.

SERVICE CEILING:
20,000 ft. (overload)

R. A. F.: HALIFAX I, II
HALIFAX series

HEAVY BOMBER

U.K.

"HALIFAX"

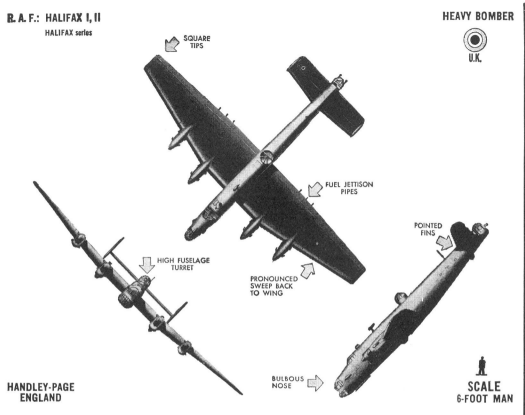

SQUARE TIPS

FUEL JETTISON PIPES

HIGH FUSELAGE TURRET

PRONOUNCED SWEEP BACK TO WING

POINTED FINS

BULBOUS NOSE

SCALE 6-FOOT MAN

HANDLEY-PAGE ENGLAND

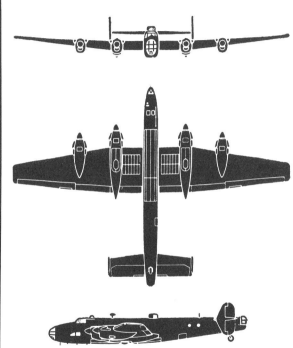

DISTINGUISHING FEATURES: Mid - wing monoplane with four in-line engines underslung. Dihedral on outer wing panels. Equi-taper on outer wing panels and square tips. Elongated fuselage. Twin fin and rudders, with V-shaped leading edges.

INTEREST: This seven-place, long-range heavy bomber can carry very large bomb loads for great distances. It was designed for production-line speed rather than air speed, and is not as fast as the Lancaster or American heavy bombers of the same type. It has been in use in the Middle East and extensively over Germany, where its "block busting" bombs have caused considerable damage. This bomber was christened by Lord Halifax, the present British Ambassador to the United States. Pilots call the aircraft the "Halibag." Maximum bomb load is approximately 11,000 lbs. The nose is currently being altered to a simple oval form, largely transparent.

SPAN: 99 ft.
LENGTH: 71 ft. 7 in.
MAX. SPEED: 262 m. p. h. at 17,750 ft.

SERVICE CEILING: 17,800 ft. (overload)

RESTRICTED

APRIL 1943
FROM DATA CURRENTLY AVAILABLE

WAR DEPARTMENT FM 30–30
NAVY DEPARTMENT BUAER 3

R. A. F.: STIRLING I, II

"STIRLING"

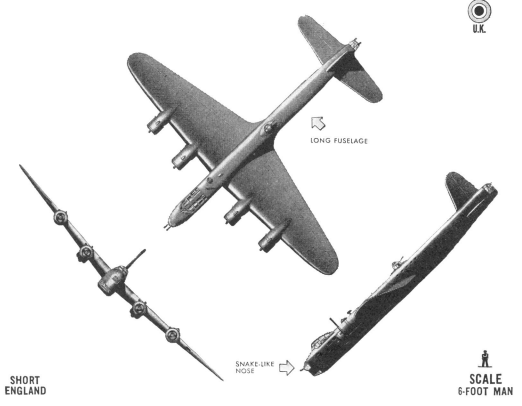

LONG FUSELAGE

SNAKE-LIKE NOSE

**SHORT
ENGLAND**

**SCALE
6-FOOT MAN**

DISTINGUISHING FEATURES: Mid - wing monoplane with four radial engines. Inboard engines underslung. Dihedral from wing roots. Wing equally tapered with sharply rounded tips. Long slab-sided fuselage with small greenhouse placed high on nose. Tall single fin-and-rudder forward of tail turret.

INTEREST: The Short "Stirling" was the first of the big British four-engined bombers to go into service, becoming operational early in 1941. It has taken part in many night raids on Germany and many daylight sorties over France. This aircraft can carry over 8 tons of bombs, one of the heaviest loads of any bomber in operation today.

SPAN: 99 ft.
LENGTH: 87 ft. 3 in.
APPROX. MAX. SPEED: 272 m. p. h. at 14,000 ft.

SERVICE CEILING:
18,000 ft. (overload)

APRIL 1943
FROM DATA CURRENTLY AVAILABLE

WAR DEPARTMENT FM 30—30
NAVY DEPARTMENT BUAER 3

RESTRICTED

R. A. F.: LANCASTER I
LANCASTER I, II

HEAVY BOMBER

U.K.

"LANCASTER"

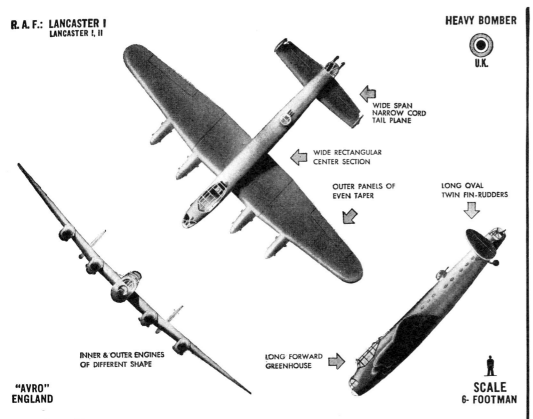

WIDE SPAN
NARROW CORD
TAIL PLANE

WIDE RECTANGULAR
CENTER SECTION

OUTER PANELS OF
EVEN TAPER

LONG OVAL
TWIN FIN-RUDDERS

INNER & OUTER ENGINES
OF DIFFERENT SHAPE

LONG FORWARD
GREENHOUSE

SCALE
6- FOOTMAN

"AVRO"
ENGLAND

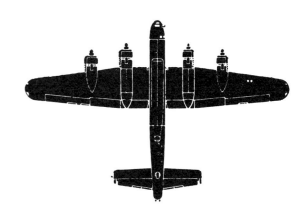

DISTINGUISHING FEATURES: Mid - wing monoplane. Slight dihedral on outer wing panels. Four in-line engines underslung. Wings equally tapered on outer panels with round tips. Long boxlike fuselage with cockpit enclosure set well forward and prominent tail turret aft. Tall oval twin fins and rudders set outboard of tail plane.

INTEREST: The existence of this 30-ton long range heavy bomber was not publicized until it participated in a daring daylight raid in 1942 on the Diesel works which were producing engines for submarines at Augsburg, Germany. Reputed to be one of the easiest of contemporary aircraft to build, it is now in large scale production. It has an outside range of nearly 3,000 miles. It can carry a bomb load of over 6 tons. This bomber carries machine guns in 4 power turrets. The Lancaster I is powered by liquid cooled in-lined engines, while the Mark II has air cooled radials.

SPAN: 102 ft.
LENGTH: 69 ft. 6 in.
MAX. SPEED: 280 m. p. h.

SERVICE CEILING:
25,800 ft.

APRIL 1943
FROM DATA CURRENTLY AVAILABLE

WAR DEPARTMENT FM 30—30
NAVY DEPARTMENT BUAER 3

TROOP GLIDER

U.K.

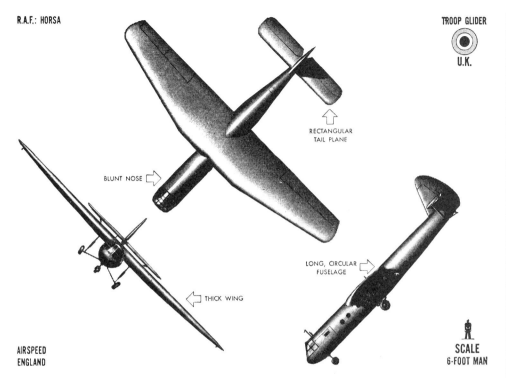

RECTANGULAR
TAIL PLANE

BLUNT NOSE

LONG, CIRCULAR
FUSELAGE

THICK WING

AIRSPEED
ENGLAND

SCALE
6-FOOT MAN

HORSA

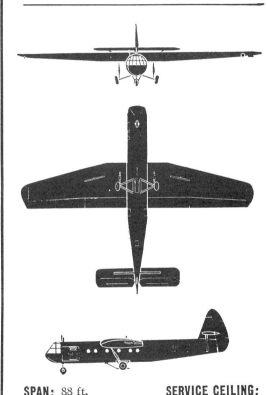

SPAN: 88 ft.

LENGTH: 67 ft.

NORMAL TOWING SPEED:

SERVICE CEILING:

RESTRICTED

DISTINGUISHING FEATURES: High-wing monoplane. Cylindrical fuselage with very long, partially glazed nose. Wing tapers on leading edge outboard of rectangular center section. Blunt wing tips. No dihedral. Straight fuselage from nose to trailing edge of wing, tapered from there to tail. Rectangular horizontal tailplane mounted above fuselage. High, pointed single fin and rudder with curved trailing edge. Fixed tricycle landing gear; main gear may be jettisoned.

INTEREST: The Horsa is one of Britain's standard troop-carrying gliders. Built mainly of wood, it is notable for being the first craft of its kind to be fitted with a tricycle landing gear. The wheels can be jettisoned after take-off and the glider landed on its skids. This would be done in an actual airborne attack to shorten the landing. Ungainly in appearance, the Horsa pairs well with its tug, the Whitley.

ANSON

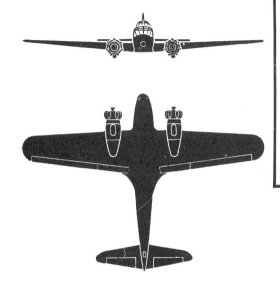

SPAN: 56 ft. 6 in.
LENGTH: 42 ft. 3 in.
MAX. SPEED: 188 m. p. h.

SERVICE CEILING:
19,000 ft.

DISTINGUISHING FEATURES: Single radial engine, low-wing monoplane. Thick, inverted gull wing with equal taper and squarish clipped tips. Prominent cockpit canopy faired into fuselage. Bell-shaped fin and rudder. Tailplane has straight edges with round tips.

INTEREST: The Master was first developed in 1936. It was adopted officially as the British Advanced Trainer when the air expansion program began. It has the typical Miles construction consisting of wood with plywood skin and thick wing section. The Master I was powered with a Rolls Royce Kestrel–XXX liquid-cooled engine. The Master II had a Bristol Mercury 20 radial engine. The present Master III is powered with a Pratt & Whitney Wasp radial engine. The Master is the only British aircraft in which the landing gear retracts backward and turns to lie flat in the wings. It is extremely maneuverable.

DISTINGUISHING FEATURES: Twin radial engine, low-wing monoplane. Wings have equal taper with round tips, and large fillet at roots. Long glazed cabin enclosure. Tapered tailplane with sharp tips. Low, rounded single fin and rudder.

INTEREST: This aircraft is now being built in Canada by Federal Aircraft Limited, and is used as an advanced trainer. Its duties consist of twin-engine training, navigational, gunnery, and bombing training. It is also used for light communications work and pilot taxi duties. During the early part of the war it carried on some operational work and scored a number of victories over faster and more heavily armed enemy aircraft.

MASTER III

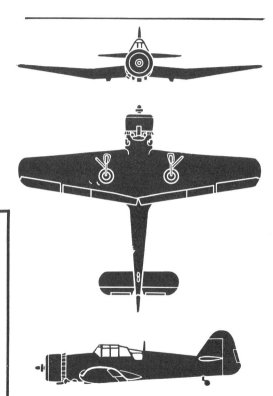

SPAN: 39 ft.
LENGTH: 29 ft. 6 in.
MAX. SPEED:

SERVICE CEILING:

RESTRICTED

GERMANY: F. W. 190A–3
F. W. 190 series

JAPAN: "FRED"

FOCKE-WULF "F. W. 190"

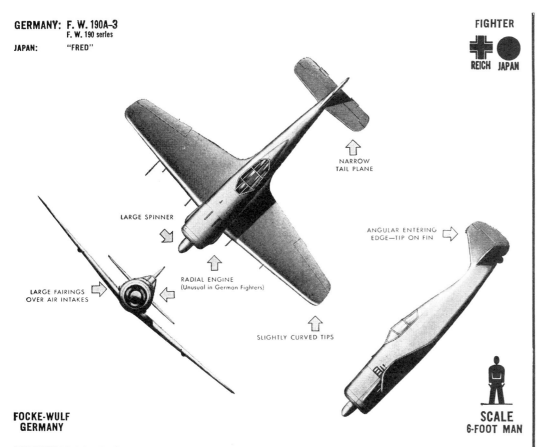

NARROW TAIL PLANE

LARGE SPINNER

ANGULAR ENTERING EDGE—TIP ON FIN

RADIAL ENGINE (Unusual in German Fighters)

LARGE FAIRINGS OVER AIR INTAKES

SLIGHTLY CURVED TIPS

SCALE 6-FOOT MAN

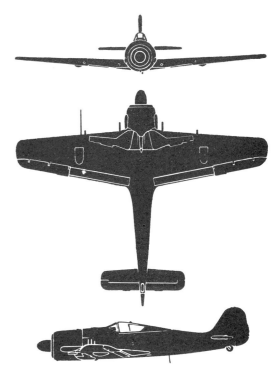

FOCKE-WULF GERMANY

DISTINGUISHING FEATURES: Short blunt nose with large spinner. Short thin tapered wings with blunt tips. Fuselage narrow aft of wings. Rectangular stabilizer and tail plane. Tall fin and rudder. Small low cockpit tapering into fuselage.

INTEREST: This is the only single-engine German fighter with a radial engine. The use of an air-cooled engine represents a radical change in German fighter philosophy. The "190" looks more like an American plane than any previous German design. First used over Europe in the summer of 1941, the "190" is now also said to be in use by the Japanese Air Force in the Southwest Pacific where it is known as "Fred."

SPAN: 34 feet 6 in.
LENGTH: 29 ft. 1 in.

MAX. SPEED: 395 m. p. h. at 17,000 ft.

SERVICE CEILING:
37,000 ft. (not loaded)
36,000 ft. (normal load)

MESSERSCHMITT "ME. 210"

GUN BLISTER
EACH SIDE

DIVE BRAKES
BOTH SURFACES

NACELLES PROJECT
WELL FORWARD

"BULGED" GREENHOUSE FORWARD

MESSERSCHMITT
GERMANY

SCALE
6-FOOT MAN

DISTINGUISHING FEATURES: Twin in-line engine, low-wing monoplane. Wing has dihedral from the roots and equal taper to small round tips. The engines extend slightly beyond the short nose. Slim tapering fuselage with high and long streamlined cockpit enclosure. Side gun blisters. Tall prominent single fin and rudder.

INTEREST: The first aircraft of this type was examined in September 1942. Some call it the German answer to the Mosquito. A maximum of 3,300 lbs. in bombs can be carried. The sides of the fuselage contain movable guns in revolving blisters. They are remotely controlled by the radio operator. The guns have a wide cone of fire. Sighting is done by means of a reflector sight.

APRIL 1943
FROM DATA CURRENTLY AVAILABLE

WAR DEPARTMENT FM 30-30
NAVY DEPARTMENT BUAER 3

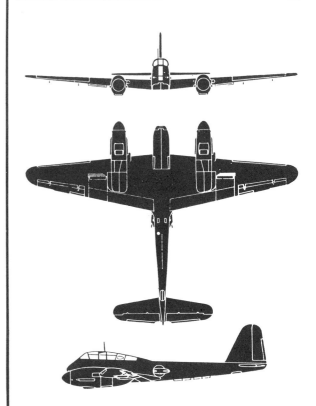

SPAN: 53 ft. 6 in.
LENGTH: 40 ft. 3 in.
MAX. SPEED: 368 m. p. h. at 20,000 ft. (as fighter)

SERVICE CEILING: 28,500 ft. (no bombs)

RESTRICTED

GERMANY: Me. 109F
Me. 109 series

JAPAN: "MIKE"

MESSERSCHMITT "ME. 109"

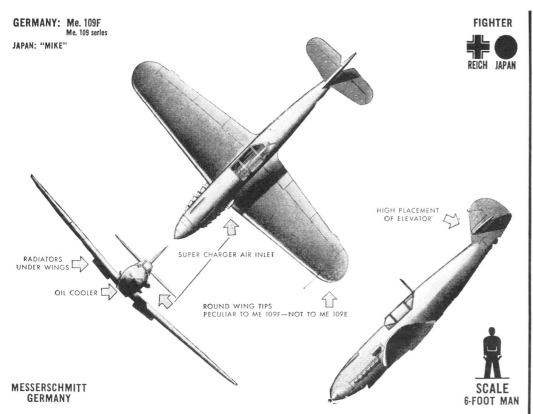

RADIATORS UNDER WINGS ⇨

OIL COOLER ⇨

SUPER CHARGER AIR INLET

ROUND WING TIPS PECULIAR TO ME 109F—NOT TO ME 109E

HIGH PLACEMENT OF ELEVATOR ⇨

SCALE 6-FOOT MAN

MESSERSCHMITT GERMANY

DISTINGUISHING FEATURES: Low - wing monoplane with single in-line engine and thick nose. Air scoops under each wing and under nose. Wings tapered with rounded tips and dihedral from roots. Stabilizer set high on small fin and rudder. Long fuselage with low cock-pit.

INTEREST: The Messerschmitts swarmed over England during the Battle of Britain and they have been in the thick of action on every front where the Luftwaffe has operated. This fighter has maneuverability, climb-ing ability, and its ceiling is higher than some of the Allied fighters sent against it. This aircraft also is used at times as a light bomber in support of ground troops and, in the Southwest Pacific where this aircraft is used by the Japs, it is known as "Mike." A high altitude version, the Me. 109G is now coming into use. It is very similar in appearance to the Me. 109F. An earlier model, the Me. 109E, has square wing tips with a span of 32 ft. 6 in. and stabilizer struts. The 109E is now obsolescent and is going out of service.

SPAN: 32 ft. 9 in.
LENGTH: 29 ft. 10 in.
MAX. SPEED: 370 m. p. h. at 22,000 ft.

SERVICE CEILING: 38,000 ft.
(with normal load, 37,000 ft.)

RESTRICTED

GERMANY: Me. 110

JAPAN: "DOC"

REICH   JAPAN

MESSERSCHMITT "ME. 110"

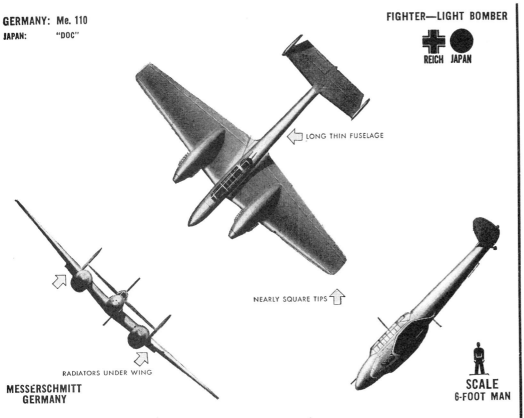

LONG THIN FUSELAGE

NEARLY SQUARE TIPS

RADIATORS UNDER WING

**MESSERSCHMITT
GERMANY**

**SCALE
6-FOOT MAN**

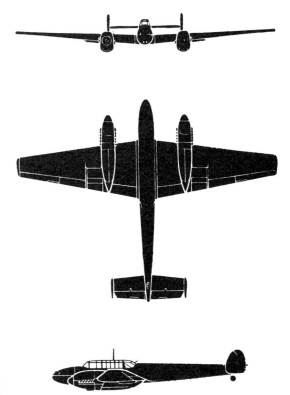

DISTINGUISHING FEATURES: Twin-engine, low-wing monoplane. Tapered wings have full dihedral and square tips. Twin in-line engines are underslung. Fuselage is slim with long cockpit enclosure. Twin fins and rudders, oval in shape with flattened bottoms, are set outboard of stabilizer and elevator.

INTEREST: The Me 110 first flew in 1938. Although it is a fast aircraft, its inferior maneuverability make it somewhat more vulnerable than the Me 109, and it is now infrequently used as a fighter on the European front. It has been used extensively, however, as a day and night fighter on the Russian front and in Libya. The Me 110 is also being used for bombing and for ground attacks. Certain reconnaissance squadrons are now equipped with them. Some long-range fighter versions are equipped with a special blister tank under the fuselage in addition to two jettisonable wing tanks.

APRIL 1943
FROM DATA CURRENTLY AVAILABLE

WAR DEPARTMENT FM 30—30
NAVY DEPARTMENT BUAER 3

SPAN: 53 ft. 11 in.
LENGTH: 40 ft. 4 in.

SERVICE CEILING:
34,000 ft. (not loaded)
32,000 ft. (normal load)

APPROX. SPEED: 350 m. p. h. at 22,000 ft.

RESTRICTED

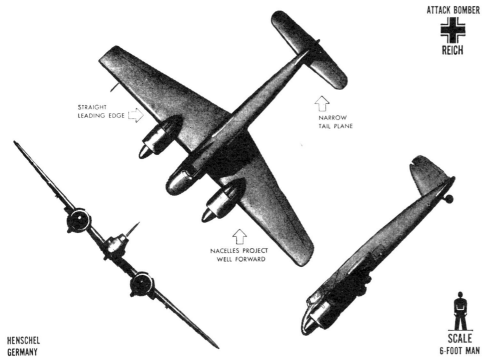

STRAIGHT LEADING EDGE

NARROW TAIL PLANE

NACELLES PROJECT WELL FORWARD

SCALE
6-FOOT MAN

HENSCHEL
GERMANY

HS. 129

DISTINGUISHING FEATURES: Twin-engine, low-wing monoplane. The two radial engines are underslung and project forward nearly as far as the nose. Wings have straight leading edge, tapered trailing edge, and blunt tips. Fuselage tapers to point at tail and has gun trough below extending slightly forward of wing. Nose is broad and slopes sharply to point from pilot's cockpit. Tailplane tapers very slightly and has round tips. Prominent single fin and rudder with broad rounded top.

INTEREST: The HS. 129 is the standard ground-attack airplane of the German Air Force. It was developed for close cooperation with the Army and is noted for its heavy armor and armament. Originally fitted with Argus air-cooled "V" engines, the HS. 129 is now fitted with Gnome-Rhone air-cooled radial engines. It may be seen with bomb rack in place of gun trough below fuselage.

SPAN: 44 ft. 6 in.
LENGTH: 33 ft. 3 in.
MAX. SPEED: 275 m. p. h. at 9,000 ft.

SERVICE CEILING: 24,500 ft. with normal load

RESTRICTED

DORNIER "DO. 26"

SWEPT BACK

HIGH
RUDDER ⇨

GULL
WING

TANDEM ⇨
ENGINES

⇩ SHALLOW
HULL

SCALE
6-FOOT MAN

**DORNIER
GERMANY**

DISTINGUISHING FEATURES: Four in-line engines in tandem pairs, propellers fore and aft. Engines are mounted on top of wings. High gull wing with tapered leading edge, straight trailing edge and blunt tips. Long flying boat hull. High triangular fin and rudder. Stabilizer and elevator set high.

INTEREST: The DO–26 is the only four-engined liquid-cooled flying boat which is ranked as a first-line plane. For recognition purposes, this aircraft is to be con-sidered as a two-engined airplane since it has only two nacelles, the four Diesel engines being mounted in tandem. It is a militarized version of an aircraft which was originally designed for Trans-Atlantic Mail Service, but completed too late for use. Its estimated range is approximately 3,470 miles. In spite of its weight (44,000 lbs.), the Germans launch the DO–26 from catapults. Its wing floats retract inward into the wings.

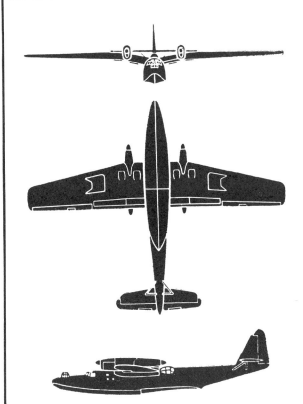

SPAN: 98 ft. 6 in.
LENGTH: 80 ft. 6 in.
MAX. SPEED: 200 m. p. h.

SERVICE CEILING:
16,000 ft.

RESTRICTED

GERMANY: Ju. 88A–6
Ju. 88 series

JAPAN: "JANICE"

MEDIUM BOMBER-FIGHTER

REICH   JAPAN

JUNKERS "JU. 88"

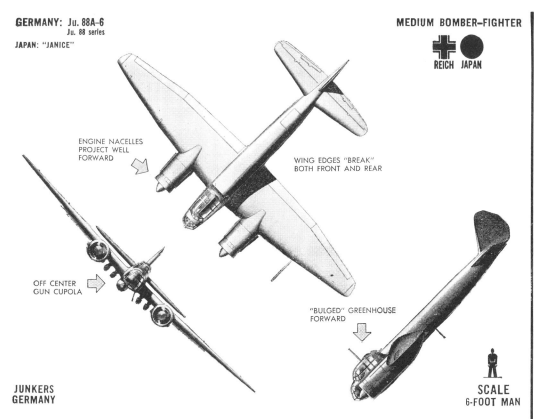

ENGINE NACELLES
PROJECT WELL
FORWARD

WING EDGES "BREAK"
BOTH FRONT AND REAR

OFF CENTER
GUN CUPOLA

"BULGED" GREENHOUSE
FORWARD

SCALE
6-FOOT MAN

JUNKERS
GERMANY

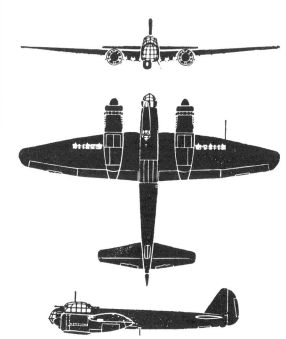

DISTINGUISHING FEATURES: Twin-engine low-wing monoplane. Heavy radial-type engine nacelles protrude well out from wing. Engines in line with nose. Narrow fuselage with off-center bomber's position under nose. Wings tapered in outer panels with rounded tips. Cockpit well forward. Tapered stabilizer and elevators with blunt tips. Single fin and rudder. Rudder projects well beyond elevators.
ITEREST: The Ju-88 is one of the chief offensive

weapons of the Nazis. In service on all fronts, it is used as a day and night fighter and for dive and level bombing of both land and sea targets. Its liquid-cooled engines resemble radials because of the circular radiators. The bomber version of this aircraft can be fitted with jettisonable rocket devices under the wings to assist in take-off. Because of the many uses to which the Ju-88 is put, there are a number of different arrangements in armament and some structural variations.

SPAN: 66 ft.
LENGTH: 47 ft.

SERVICE CEILING:
30,000 ft. (no load)
19,000 ft. (normal load)

MAX. SPEED: 287 m. p. h. at 14,000 ft. (no load)
269 m. p. h. at 14,000 ft. (loaded)

APRIL 1943
FROM DATA CURRENTLY AVAILABLE

WAR DEPARTMENT FM 30—30
NAVY DEPARTMENT BUAER

RESTRICTED

GERMANY: He. 111K
He. 111 series

MEDIUM BOMBER

✠ **REICH**

HEINKEL "HE. 111"

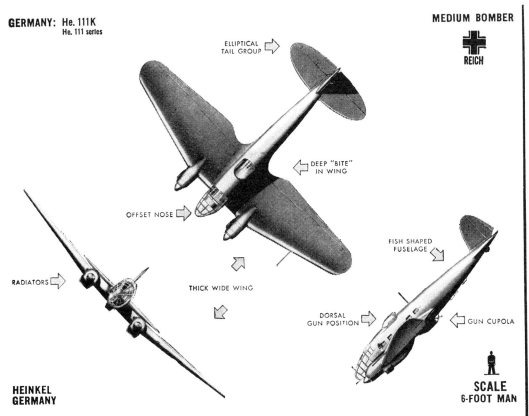

ELLIPTICAL TAIL GROUP

DEEP "BITE" IN WING

OFFSET NOSE

FISH SHAPED FUSELAGE

RADIATORS

THICK WIDE WING

DORSAL GUN POSITION

GUN CUPOLA

HEINKEL GERMANY

SCALE 6-FOOT MAN

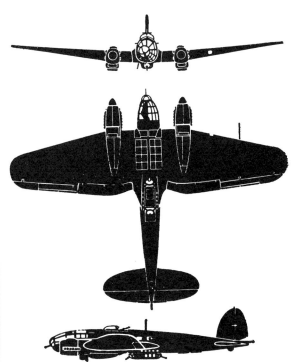

DISTINGUISHING FEATURES: Twin-engine low-wing monoplane with pronounced taper on leading edge of wing. Slightly tapered trailing edge, with "bite" at wing roots. Twin in-line engines underslung and protruding forward nearly as far as nose. Fuselage broken by ventral gun position just aft of wings, and by dorsal gun position above wings. Large transparent nose is off center to allow pilot vision past nose gunner. Large curved fin and rudder with cut-out to allow free elevator movement. Large elliptical stabilizer and elevator.

INTEREST: This bomber has undergone continuous improvement since it first appeared in 1935. The latest version, He 111 H-6 carries bombs or 2 torpedoes and has been used against Russian-bound convoys and in the Mediterranean. The aircraft is sometimes provided with rocket or some other type of "assisted take-off" equipment.

SPAN: 73 ft. 11 in.
LENGTH: 53 feet 8 in.

MAX. SPEED: 255 m. p. h. at 16,000 ft.

SERVICE CEILING:
31,500 feet (not loaded)
26,500 feet (normal load)

APRIL 1943
FROM DATA CURRENTLY AVAILABLE

WAR DEPARTMENT FM 30–30
NAVY DEPARTMENT BUAER 3

GERMANY: He. 115K

TORPEDO BOMBER—RECONNAISSANCE

✚
REICH

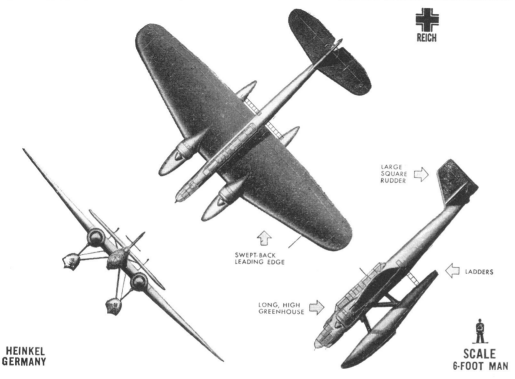

LARGE
SQUARE
RUDDER ➡

SWEPT-BACK
LEADING EDGE

⬆ LADDERS

LONG, HIGH
GREENHOUSE ➡

HEINKEL
GERMANY

SCALE
6-FOOT MAN

HEINKEL "HE. 115"

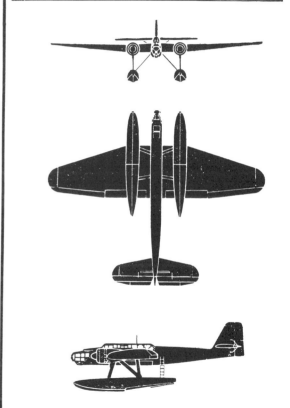

DISTINGUISHING FEATURES: Twin-engined, mid-wing monoplane with twin floats. Wings have pronounced taper on leading edge and rounded tips. Twin radial engines in wings above floats. Long slim fuselage with long cockpit enclosure and transparent nose. Tall angular single fin and rudder. Stabilizer has tapered leading edge, curved tips; elevators have "V" cut-out.

INTEREST: The He 115 has undergone many revisions since it first flew as a mail plane in 1937. The He 115

K–2, which appeared in 1939, is used for torpedo dropping, mine laying, and long range overseas reconnaissance. It was the first plane to lay the widely publicized German magnetic mine, and can be equipped also for laying smoke screens and spraying gas. By reinforcing the floats, this aircraft has been operated from snow-covered airdromes, and floats can be equipped with "skates" for landing on ice. One interesting feature of the He 115 is the installation of the fixed machine guns, one in the rear of each engine nacelle, firing aft.

APRIL 1943
FROM DATA CURRENTLY AVAILABLE

WAR DEPARTMENT FM 30–30
NAVY DEPARTMENT BUAER 3

SPAN: 72 ft. 10 in.
LENGTH: 56 ft. 8 in.

MAX. SPEED: 206 m. p. h. at 11,500 ft.

SERVICE CEILING:
27,000 ft. (not loaded)
18,500 ft. (with load)

RESTRICTED

FOCKE-WULF "F.W. 189"

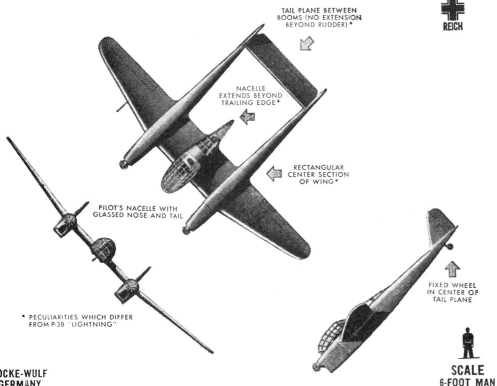

TAIL PLANE BETWEEN BOOMS (NO EXTENSION BEYOND RUDDER) *

NACELLE EXTENDS BEYOND TRAILING EDGE *

RECTANGULAR CENTER SECTION OF WING *

PILOT'S NACELLE WITH GLASSED NOSE AND TAIL

FIXED WHEEL IN CENTER OF TAIL PLANE

* PECULIARITIES WHICH DIFFER FROM P-38 "LIGHTNING"

FOCKE-WULF GERMANY

SCALE 6-FOOT MAN

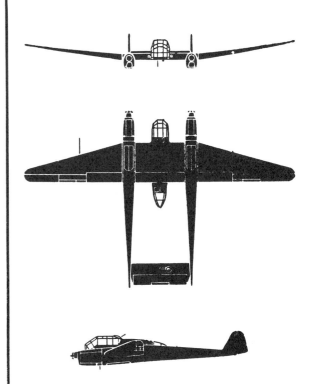

DISTINGUISHING FEATURES: Low-wing monoplane with two in-line engines. Engines extend forward of fuselage nose. Fuselage is well glazed, and extends to a point aft of trailing edge of wing. Wing is tapered on leading edge in outer panels with sharply rounded tips and has straight trailing edge. Engine nacelles extend aft as twin booms ending in twin fins and rudders. Rectangular stabilizer and elevator set between booms.

INTEREST: Called the "Flying Eye," these aircraft are used for army cooperation, ground attack, communications, advanced training, and as supply transports and ambulances. The normal crew is three. Take-off and landing runs are short and the landing gear is sufficiently robust for front-line flying fields of poor surface quality. It has proved extremely useful on the Russian front.

SPAN: 60 ft. 5 in.
LENGTH: 39 ft. 5 in.
MAX. SPEED: 210 m. p. h. at 8,530 ft.

SERVICE CEILING: 27,550 ft (normal load)

RESTRICTED

BLOHM & VOSS "HA. 138"

BROAD TAILPLANE ←

TURRET ←

SHORT BOOMS ←

PROJECTING →

HIGH ←

WIDELY-SPACED ENGINES →

FIXED →

TURRET →

SHORT HULL ←

SCALE 6-FOOT MAN

BLOHM AND VOSS
GERMANY

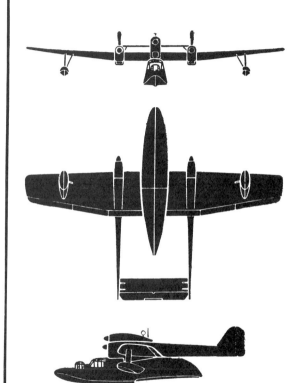

DISTINGUISHING FEATURES: High-wing monoplane with three in-line engines. Hull has single step and projects well in front of wings. Wings are tapered slightly on outer sections with raking tips. Fixed wing floats. Engines mounted on top of wing, the center one being noticeably higher. Nacelles of outboard engines extend to form twin tail booms ending in twin fins and rudders, with marked taper on leading edges. Rectangular stabilizers set between booms.

INTEREST: Used for general reconnaissance work and bombing, this flying boat carries a crew of five or six. A slow ship, common fault of all flying boats, this plane cruises at 152 m. p. h. with a 1,000 pound bomb load, and has a range of 1,425 miles. One of the older type German flying boats, the BV 138 is used primarily for observation reconnaissance over sea areas. An unusual feature is that some sub-types are fitted with a power operated gun turret in the nose, mounting a 15-mm gun.

SPAN: 88 ft. 7 in.
LENGTH: 65 ft. 5 in.
MAX. SPEED: 170 m. p. h. at sea level

SERVICE CEILING: 18,000 ft. (normal load)

RESTRICTED

GERMANY: Ju. 87B
Ju. 87 series

ITALY: BREDA 201

JAPAN: "IRENE"

DIVE BOMBER

REICH   ITALY   JAPAN

JUNKERS "JU. 87" "STUKA"

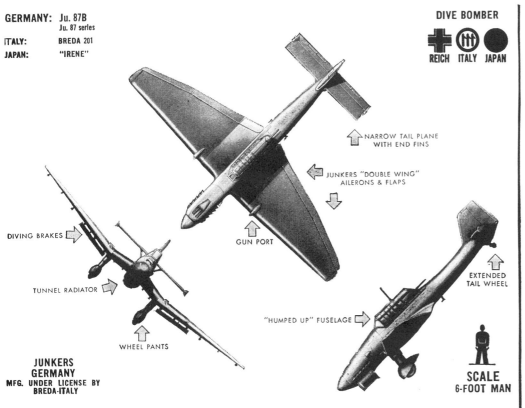

NARROW TAIL PLANE
WITH END FINS

JUNKERS "DOUBLE WING"
AILERONS & FLAPS

DIVING BRAKES

TUNNEL RADIATOR

GUN PORT

WHEEL PANTS

**JUNKERS
GERMANY**
MFG. UNDER LICENSE BY
BREDA-ITALY

EXTENDED
TAIL WHEEL

"HUMPED UP" FUSELAGE

SCALE
6-FOOT MAN

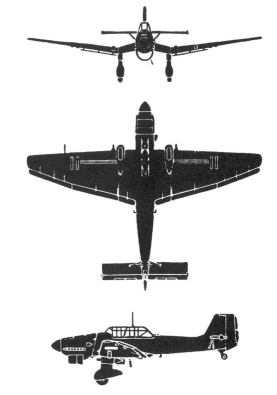

DISTINGUISHING FEATURES: Low inverted gull-wing monoplane, with in-line engine. Long nose and large spinner. Big rounded radiator below nose. Fixed landing gear with wheel fairings. Prominent square cut single fin and rudder with taper to leading edge of fin. Braced rectangular stabilizer and elevator.

INTEREST: One of the most widely used German planes, the "Stuka" has proved to be extremely vulnerable. Hundreds of these planes have been shot down by

Allied air pilots and by A. A. fire. During the fighting in Poland and the Low Countries, this dive bomber earned a reputation as ugly as its appearance. A later model, the JU 87D is now in use (Photo B). It has a modified cockpit cover and a less conspicuous radiator. The plane is also manufactured by Breda in Italy and is then known as the BR 201. A captured report indicates that one modification, the Ju 87C–1, has jettisonable undercarriage that can be dropped to get increased speed in an emergency.

SPAN: 45 ft. 4 in.
LENGTH: 36 ft. 6 in.

SERVICE CEILING:
30,000 ft. (not loaded)
25,000 ft. (normal load)

MAX. SPEED: 225 m. p. h. at 15,000 (with load)
245 m. p. h. at 15,000 (bombs unloaded)

APRIL 1943
FROM DATA CURRENTLY AVAILABLE

WAR DEPARTMENT FM 30
NAVY DEPARTMENT BUAER

RESTRICTED

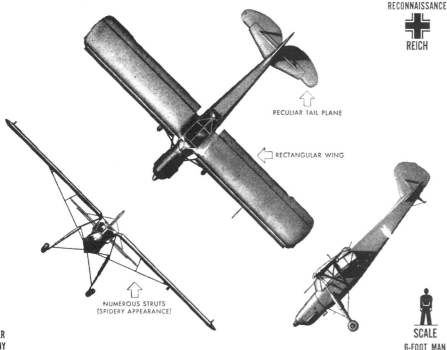

PECULIAR TAIL PLANE

RECTANGULAR WING

NUMEROUS STRUTS
(SPIDERY APPEARANCE)

SCALE
6-FOOT MAN

**FIESELER
GERMANY**

DISTINGUISHING FEATURES: Single-engine, high-wing monoplane. Slim nose and fuselage. Straight, rectangular-shaped wings braced with **V** struts. Large glazed canopy. The elevators are curved with a large cut-out in the center at the trailing edge. Fixed landing gear with long stork-like legs.

INTEREST: The "Storch" is used primarily for light communications work. It is about the nearest approach to an autogyro that is possible with fixed wings. It can maintain flight at 31 m. p. h. and lands at 25 m. p. h. The maximum landing run using brakes is only 30 yards. The plane is equipped with full-span leading edge slots which may be of a fixed or movable type. Large camber-changing flaps aid slow landings. This aircraft received mention for a landing in a small public park in Paris. General Montgomery used a captured "Storch" for some time in Libya.

Fl. 156

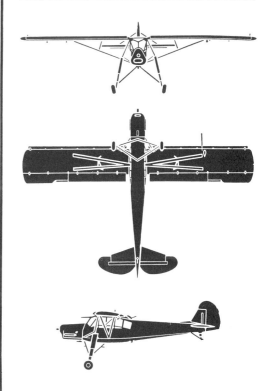

SPAN: 46 ft. 10 in.
LENGTH: 32 ft. 6 in.
MAX. SPEED: 145 m. p. h. at 3,000 ft.

SERVICE CEILING:
17,000 ft.

RESTRICTED

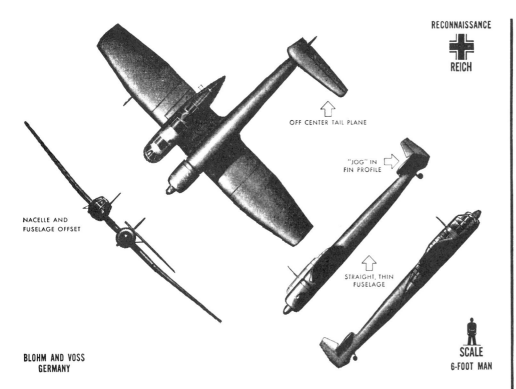

OFF CENTER TAIL PLANE

"JOG" IN FIN PROFILE

STRAIGHT, THIN FUSELAGE

NACELLE AND FUSELAGE OFFSET

SCALE 6-FOOT MAN

BLOHM AND VOSS GERMANY

B. V. 141

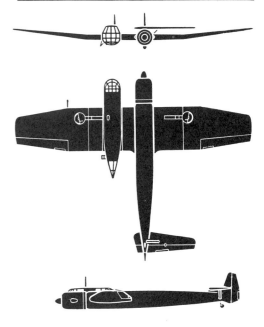

DISTINGUISHING FEATURES: Single - engine, midwing, asymmetrical monoplane. Wing has long, straight center section with tapered outer section and blunt tips. The engine is housed in main fuselage to the left of the cabin, which projects beyond both leading and trailing edges of wing. Horizontal stabilizer extends to the left side of the fuselage with only small stub on the right side. Single fin and rudder is small and angular.

INTEREST: The B. V. 141 was designed for tactical reconnaissance and may be in service in small numbers. A very odd-looking aircraft, its principal advantage is in visibility obtained by the unusual design.

SPAN: 60 ft. (est.) **SERVICE CEILING:**
LENGTH: 45 ft. (est.)
APPROX. SPEED: 280 m. p. h. at 16,000 ft.

RESTRICTED

"ARADO 196"

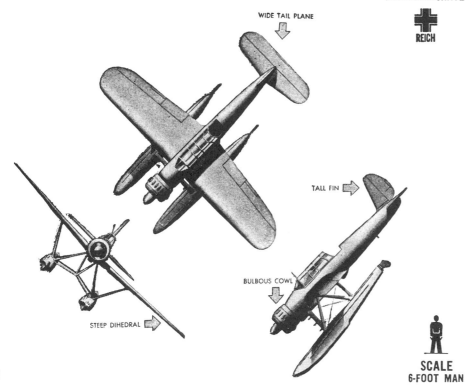

WIDE TAIL PLANE

TALL FIN

BULBOUS COWL

STEEP DIHEDRAL

SCALE
6-FOOT MAN

**ARADO
GERMANY**

DISTINGUISHING FEATURES: Single radial engine, low-wing monoplane with twin floats. There is also a single-float model with small wing-tip floats (Photo B.) Wing has full dihedral, with slight taper on trailing edge and rounded tips. Stabilizer is tapered on leading edge with rounded tips.

INTEREST: The Arado first attracted attention by its association with the Graf Spee action in December 1939.

One was carried on the German battleship but failed to take off at any time during the battle against the British cruisers. The Bismarck carried several Arados, which took off to attack the Catalinas after these American-made flying boats had spotted the German warship. Operating from bases along the French coast, AR 196's have been used to harass antisub patrols of the British Coastal Command, and against light naval vessels.

APRIL 1943
FROM DATA CURRENTLY AVAILABLE

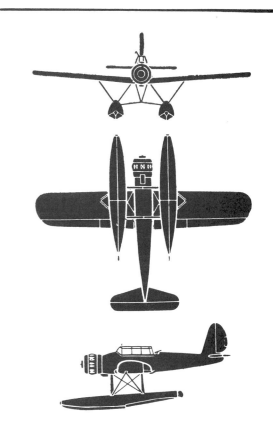

SPAN: 41 ft.
LENGTH: 36 ft. 1 in.
MAX. SPEED: 195 m. p. h. at 3,000 ft.

SERVICE CEILING:
21,500 ft.

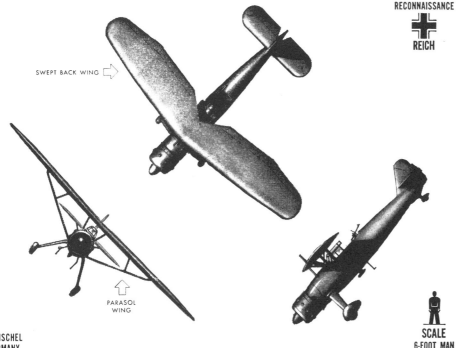

SWEPT BACK WING ⇨

⬆ PARASOL WING

SCALE
6-FOOT MAN

**HENSCHEL
GERMANY**

DISTINGUISHING FEATURES: Single radial engine monoplane with parasol wing. Wing has an irregular swept-back appearance with a large **V** cut-out in center of trailing edge. Wing is supported above fuselage by **N**-shaped struts. It is braced by **V** struts. Cylindrical fuselage tapers rearward. Cockpit semi-enclosed. Tailplane is straight with round tips and is mounted halfway up fin. It is strut braced. Fixed cantilever landing gear with wheel pants.

INTEREST: The Henschel Army cooperation monoplane came into service in 1936. The power plant is a Bramo Fafnir 323 air-cooled radial engine rated at 940 horsepower at 12,000 feet. This plane is now obsolescent but will remain in use in decreasing numbers for various duties. It can be used as a glider tug.

NOV. 1943
FROM DATA CURRENTLY AVAILABLE

SUPPLEMENT ONE

WAR DEPARTMENT FM 30—30
NAVY DEPARTMENT BUAER 3

HS. 126

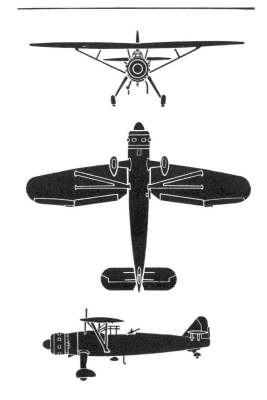

SPAN: 47 ft. 7 in.
LENGTH: 35 ft. 8 in.
MAX. SPEED: 230 m. p. h. at 15,000 ft.

SERVICE CEILING:
27,000 ft.

RESTRICTED

GERMANY: F. W. 200K

HEAVY BOMBER—TRANSPORT

✠
REICH

FOCKE-WULF "F.W. 200"

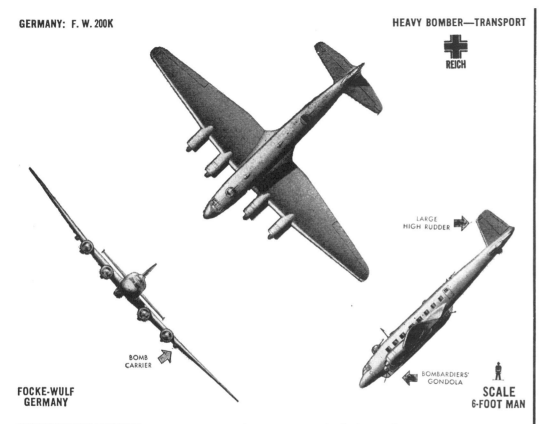

LARGE
HIGH RUDDER →

BOMB
CARRIER ⬈

**FOCKE-WULF
GERMANY**

← BOMBARDIERS'
GONDOLA

**SCALE
6-FOOT MAN**

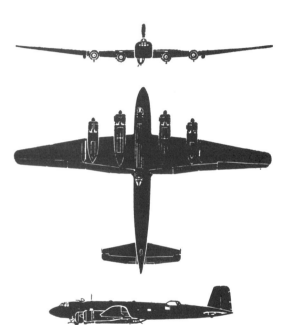

DISTINGUISHING FEATURES: Low-wing monoplane with four radial engines. Tapered wing has wide span and small round tips. Fuselage is long and tapering with long offset bomb compartment on under side. Large fin and rudder with blunt top. Tapered stabilizer and elevators have rounded tips.

INTEREST: Used extensively over the North Atlantic, this 6-place bomber carries out long-range reconnaissance, mine-laying, and convoy attacks. Against Russian-bound convoys, it has been used as a torpedo plane. Known as the "Kurier," this aircraft is a military adaptation of the "Condor," a civil transport, and this accounts for the addition of the long off-center bomb compartment under the fuselage. German submarine "Wolf Packs" are frequently in radio communication with the "Kuriers," which inform them of the courses and location of Allied convoys.

SPAN: 108 ft.
LENGTH: 78 ft.

SERVICE CEILING:
30,000 ft. (not loaded)
21,500 ft. (fully loaded)

MAX. SPEED: 235 m. p. h. at 13,000 ft. (loaded)
250 m. p. h. at 13,000 ft. (bombs unloaded)

APRIL 1943
FROM DATA CURRENTLY AVAILABLE

WAR DEPARTMENT FM 30—30
NAVY DEPARTMENT BUAER 3

JUNKERS "JU. 90"

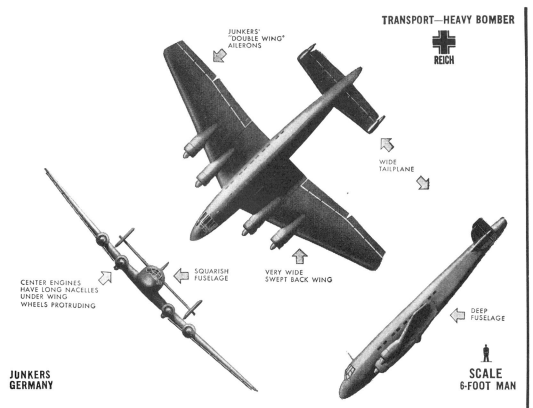

JUNKERS' "DOUBLE WING" AILERONS

WIDE TAILPLANE

SQUARISH FUSELAGE

VERY WIDE SWEPT BACK WING

CENTER ENGINES HAVE LONG NACELLES UNDER WING WHEELS PROTRUDING

DEEP FUSELAGE

JUNKERS GERMANY

SCALE 6-FOOT MAN

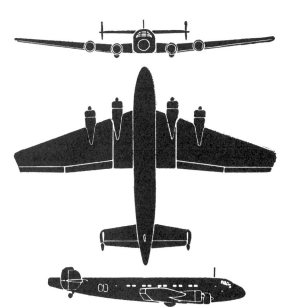

DISTINGUISHING FEATURES: Low-wing monoplane with four engines (radial or in-line). Wings are broad and decidedly swept-back with raked tips and fitted with typical Junkers "double wing" ailerons and flaps. Engine nacelles are staggered. Fuselage is broad and long with ventral line swept up to tail. Stabilizer set forward and high with equal taper on both edges. Twin fins and rudders set outboard of stabilizer.

INTEREST: Formerly Germany's largest land plane. This transport carries a crew of five and accommodates forty soldiers. A larger type of Junkers transport, known as the Ju. 290, is coming into limited use. The maximum range of this aircraft is 1,960 miles at 200 miles per hour. In addition to troop carrying and glider towing, the Ju. 90 can be pressed into service as a bomber, provision being made for stowage of a maximum bomb load of 7,700 pounds. The model having in-line engines is referred to as the "New Ju. 90."

SPAN: 115 ft. 6 in.
LENGTH: 85 ft.

SERVICE CEILING:
radial engines, 15,000 ft.
in-line engines, 24,000 ft.

MAX. SPEED: radial engines, 218 m. p. h. at 3,500 ft.
in-line engines, 260 m. p. h. at 15,000 ft.

RESTRICTED

HEINKEL "HE. 177"

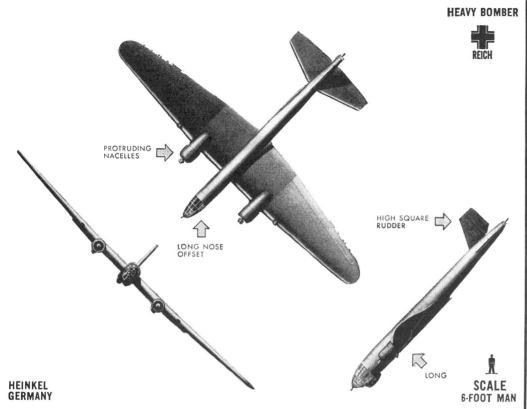

PROTRUDING NACELLES ➡

⬆ LONG NOSE OFFSET

HIGH SQUARE RUDDER ➡

⬅ LONG

SCALE 6-FOOT MAN

HEINKEL GERMANY

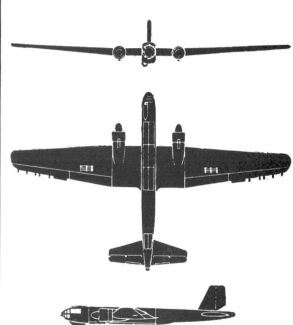

DISTINGUISHING FEATURES: Mid-wing monoplane with two radial-type engine nacelles. Wings tapered on outer panels. Long fuselage with rounded nose projecting far beyond engine nacelles. Single fin and rudder, large and angular as also are the stabilizer and elevators.

INTEREST: This aircraft became operational late in 1941. Designed primarily as a long-range "anti-blockade" aircraft, the He 177 may be employed also for short and medium range bombing, dive bombing, mine laying, torpedo dropping, and reconnaissance. A unique feature of this bomber is that each of its two engine nacelles contains really two engines geared to drive a single four blade propeller. The landing gear under each nacelle consists of 2 wheels which apparently retract spanwise and in opposite directions into the wings. Reports refer to a special high altitude version with pressure cabin.

SPAN: approx. 103 ft.
LENGTH: approx. 65 ft.
MAX. SPEED: 300 m. p. h. at 18,000 ft. (est.)

SERVICE CEILING: 23,500 ft.

APRIL 1943
FROM DATA CURRENTLY AVAILABLE

WAR DEPARTMENT FM 30-30
NAVY DEPARTMENT BUAER 3

GERMANY: Do. 217 E–2
Do. 217 series

HEAVY BOMBER

REICH

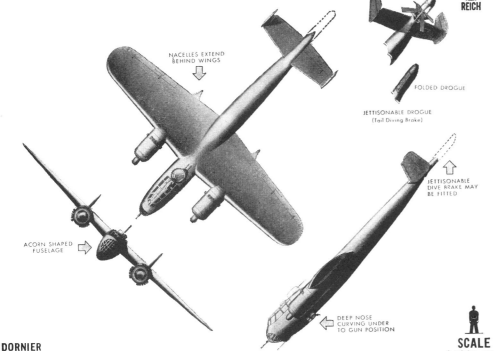

NACELLES EXTEND
BEHIND WINGS

FOLDED DROGUE

JETTISONABLE DROGUE
(Tail Diving Brake)

JETTISONABLE
DIVE BRAKE MAY
BE FITTED

ACORN SHAPED
FUSELAGE

DEEP NOSE
CURVING UNDER
TO GUN POSITION

SCALE
6-FOOT MAN

DORNIER
GERMANY

DISTINGUISHING FEATURES: Twin-engine, shoulder-wing monoplane. Short tapered wings with round tips. No dihedral. In side view, a long thin fuselage with thick nose. Dorsal turret in rear of cockpit. Twin fins and rudders set outboard of stabilizer.
INTEREST: This aircraft was introduced during the first part of 1942. It is used for level precision bombing and has also been in action as a torpedo bomber against convoys. In addition, this Dornier operates as a dive bomber and for this purpose may carry a novel "umbrella"-type jettisonable diving brake in its tail, used to slow its speed. The Do 217's are very formidable airplanes and it takes the most modern of fighters to deal with them. They are the current Dornier bomber, the older Do 17Z being obsolete. Several modifications differing somewhat in detail are in use.

APRIL 1943
FROM DATA CURRENTLY AVAILABLE

WAR DEPARTMENT FM 30—30
NAVY DEPARTMENT BUAER 3

DORNIER "DO. 217"

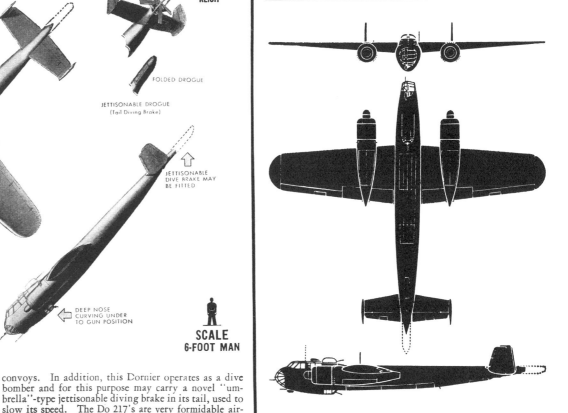

SPAN: 62 ft. 5 in.
LENGTH: 56 ft. 6 in.

SERVICE CEILING:
29,000 ft.
(with normal load, 22,500 ft.)

APPROX. SPEED: 325 m. p. h. at 17,000 ft.

RESTRICTED

D. F. S. 230

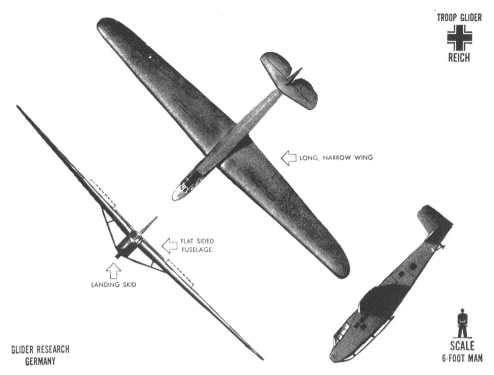

LONG, NARROW WING

FLAT SIDED FUSELAGE

LANDING SKID

SCALE
6-FOOT MAN

GLIDER RESEARCH
GERMANY

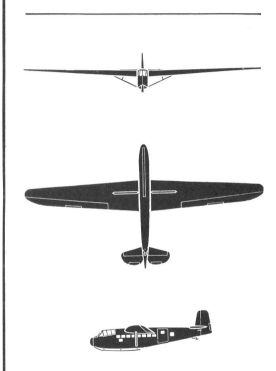

DISTINGUISHING FEATURES: High-wing monoplane braced with single struts. Wing is long and narrow with slight taper on leading edge, tapered trailing edge, and small rounded tips. Fuselage long and narrow in plan and has straight top. Cross-section is rectangular. Tailplane has tapered leading edge with round tips and curved trailing edge with **V** cut-out. Tall, single fin and rudder is slightly tapered with blunt top.

INTEREST: The D. F. S. 230 is one of Germany's standard gliders and was used in the occupation of Crete. The optimum gliding speed of this glider after release is approximately 70 m. p. h. Its landing speed in still air is from 35 to 40 m. p. h. It is a 10-seater of simple design.

SPAN: 72 ft. 4 in.   **SERVICE CEILING:**

LENGTH: 37 ft. 6 in.

NORMAL TOWING SPEED: 110 m. p. h.

RESTRICTED

NOV. 1943
FROM DATA CURRENTLY AVAILABLE

SUPPLEMENT ONE [WAR DEPARTMENT FM 30—30
NAVY DEPARTMENT BUAER 3

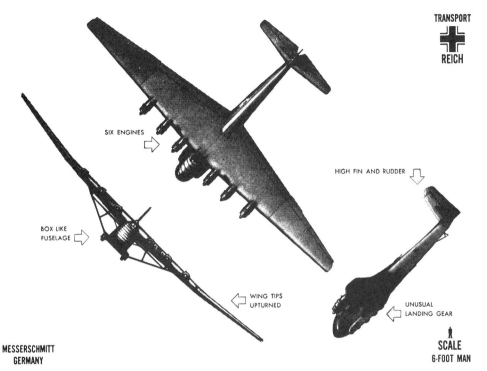

SIX ENGINES ➡

HIGH FIN AND RUDDER ⬇

BOX LIKE
FUSELAGE ➡

WING TIPS
UPTURNED ⬅

UNUSUAL
LANDING GEAR ⬅

SCALE
6-FOOT MAN

MESSERSCHMITT
GERMANY

ME. 323

DISTINGUISHING FEATURES: Six-engine, high-wing monoplane. Very long strut-braced wings are tapered to small, squarish tips. Center section is very thick and has no dihedral. Long outer panels have marked dihedral. Nose-heavy, humpback fuselage tapers sharply aft of the wing. Landing gear consists of five wheels in tandem under each side of forward fuselage. Tailplane resembles wing in plan with cut-out in elevators. Extremely tall, narrow single fin and rudder has slightly tapered edges and round top.

INTEREST: The Me. 323 is a modified, powered version of the Me. 321 "Gigant" glider. During the final stages of the Tunisian campaign, P–40 "Warhawks" completely destroyed a large formation of these giants attempting to land supplies for the besieged German troops. With a full military load of 130 troops or about 40,000 pounds of cargo, some sort of assisted take-off, either a tug or rockets, is believed to be used. The nose of the fuselage is made up of two very large doors which allow loading of heavy equipment.

SPAN: 181 ft.

LENGTH: 93 ft. 4 in.

APPROX. SPEED: 195 m. p. h. at 13,000 ft.

SERVICE CEILING:
21,000 ft.

RESTRICTED

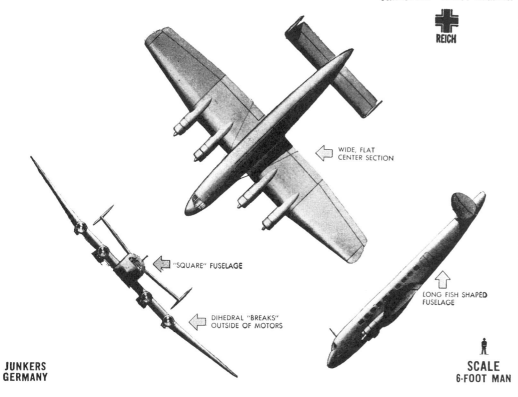

TRANSPORT—HEAVY BOMBER

✚ REICH

JUNKERS "JU. 290"

WIDE, FLAT CENTER SECTION

"SQUARE" FUSELAGE

DIHEDRAL "BREAKS" OUTSIDE OF MOTORS

LONG FISH SHAPED FUSELAGE

SCALE 6-FOOT MAN

JUNKERS
GERMANY

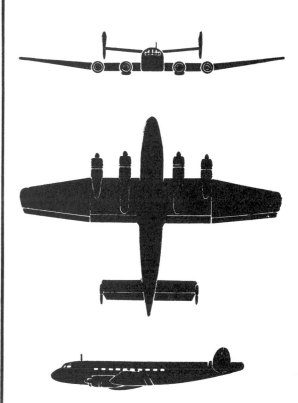

DISTINGUISHING FEATURES: Low-wing monoplane with four sharply projecting radial engines. Wing has rectangular center section with equally tapered outer section and raking tips. Wing is nearly amidships of heavy fuselage which has horizontal dorsal and curving ventral line and a cross section which is flat underneath and rounded above. Twin fins and rudders are an oval in form and are set outboard of rectangular stabilizer which is set high and forward and has pronounced dihedral.

INTEREST: The Junkers Ju. 290 is a modified version of the Ju. 90, with redesigned wings and tail. It has a range of about 1,700 miles at 200 miles per hour and has been reported to have a gross weight of over 90,000 pounds and to carry about 22,000 pounds of cargo. This enormous airplane is now coming into limited service.

SPAN: 137 ft. 6 in.
LENGTH: 90 ft.
APPROX. MAX. SPEED: 270 m. p. h. at 17,000 ft.

SERVICE CEILING: about 22,000 ft.

APRIL 1943
FROM DATA CURRENTLY AVAILABLE

WAR DEPARTMENT FM 30-30
NAVY DEPARTMENT BUAER 3

RESTRICTED

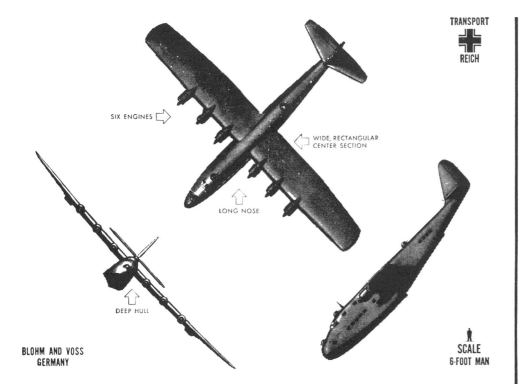

SIX ENGINES ⟹

⟸ WIDE, RECTANGULAR CENTER SECTION

⬆ LONG NOSE

⬆ DEEP HULL

BLOHM AND VOSS
GERMANY

🚶 SCALE 6-FOOT MAN

B. V. 222

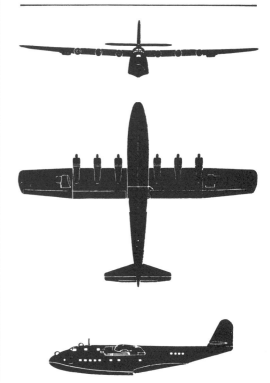

DISTINGUISHING FEATURES: Six-engine, high-wing monoplane. Inner sections of wings are straight while outer panels taper slightly to rather blunt tips. The two-step hull is long and deep with straight sides. Tall, single fin and rudder has tapered leading edge with curved trailing edge. Stabilizer is set on fin above fuselage. Wing tip floats retract inward into wing.

INTEREST: The B. V. 222 is probably the largest aircraft, excluding gliders, produced for the German Air Force since the outbreak of the war. The number of these aircraft in service is likely to be small. This flying boat is used as a long-range transport and patrol plane and carries a crew of about 10. The seating capacity is believed to be about 65 men.

SPAN: 150 ft.   **SERVICE CEILING:**
LENGTH: 115 ft.
MAX. SPEED: 240 m. p. h. at 15,000 ft. (est.)

RESTRICTED

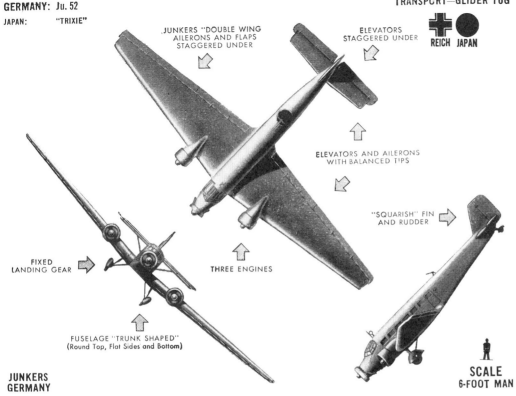

JUNKERS "DOUBLE WING" AILERONS AND FLAPS STAGGERED UNDER

ELEVATORS STAGGERED UNDER

REICH JAPAN

ELEVATORS AND AILERONS WITH BALANCED TIPS

"SQUARISH" FIN AND RUDDER

FIXED LANDING GEAR

THREE ENGINES

FUSELAGE "TRUNK SHAPED" (Round Top, Flat Sides and Bottom)

JUNKERS GERMANY

SCALE 6-FOOT MAN

JUNKERS "JU. 52"

DISTINGUISHING FEATURES: Low-wing three-engined monoplane. Wing has equal taper on both edges with square tips. Outer engines diverge slightly. Note Junkers "Double-wing" construction. Fixed landing gear. Heavy fuselage. Large angular fin and rudder and wide angular stabilizer.

INTEREST: The most widely used German transport plane, the Ju 52, although old-fashioned in design, is one of the most efficient troop and cargo carriers in operation. The Germans used it for carrying paratroops in their invasion of Holland, Norway, and Crete. More recently it has played a prominent part in carrying reinforcements to the German garrisons in Tunis. It also serves as a glider tug. In troop transport work these planes carry from 14 to 20 men, with equipment; as a paratroop transport, it can accommodate from 10 to 14 men. A seaplane version is identical apart from having twin pontoons.

SPAN: 96 ft.
LENGTH: 62 ft.

SERVICE CEILING:
21,000 ft. (without load)
16,000 ft. (max. load)

MAX. SPEED: 165 m. p. h. at sea level

"GOTHA 242"

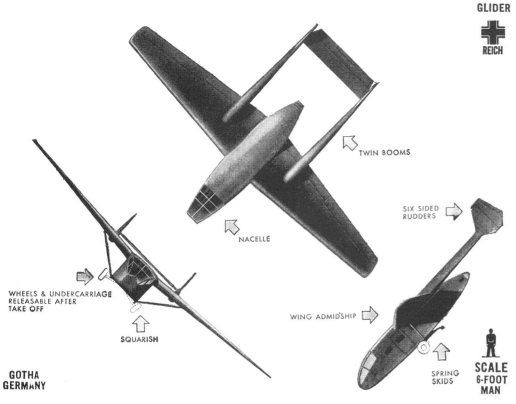

TWIN BOOMS

NACELLE

SIX SIDED RUDDERS

WING ADMID'SHIP

WHEELS & UNDERCARRIAGE RELEASABLE AFTER TAKE OFF

SQUARISH

SPRING SKIDS

SCALE 6-FOOT MAN

GOTHA GERMANY

DISTINGUISHING FEATURES: High-wing, twin-boom monoplane. Wing equally tapered with square tips. Fuselage wide and deep with square cross section. Long massive nose. Twin booms support rectangular stabilizer and twin fins and rudders of angular outline.

INTEREST: This glider is normally towed by one Junkers Ju 52 transport. The glider flies about 15 feet above the tug in order to keep clear of the slip-stream and to avoid stalling the tug by pulling its tail down. It carries 2 pilots and 21 soldiers or freight (maximum freight capacity is 5,300 pounds). It lands on three spring skids, the forward one retracting during flight. There are two powered versions of this glider, one apparently with radial engines and the other with int line engines. Reports from the Russian front state that these gliders can transport field artillery, moving as many as 20 batteries in one morning.

APRIL 1943
FROM DATA CURRENTLY AVAILABLE

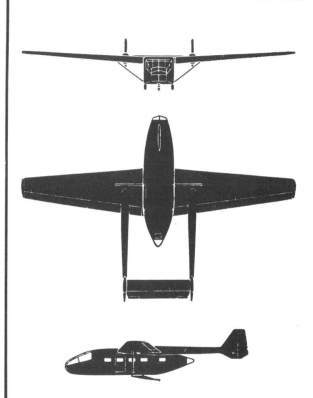

SPAN: 79 ft.
LENGTH: 52 ft. 6 in.
MAXIMUM TOWING SPEED: 149 m. p. h.

RESTRICTED

"NATE" TYPE 97 F

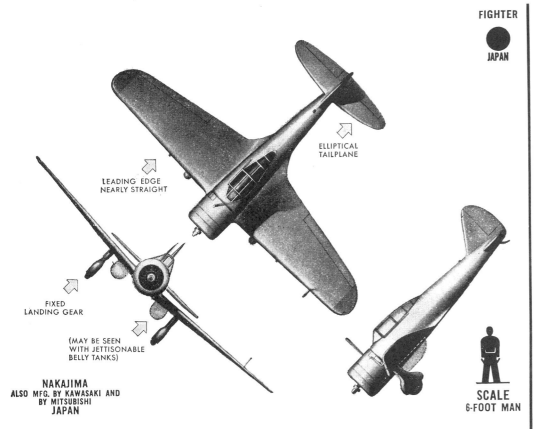

ELLIPTICAL
TAILPLANE

LEADING EDGE
NEARLY STRAIGHT

FIXED
LANDING GEAR

(MAY BE SEEN
WITH JETTISONABLE
BELLY TANKS)

NAKAJIMA
ALSO MFG. BY KAWASAKI AND
BY MITSUBISHI
JAPAN

SCALE
6-FOOT MAN

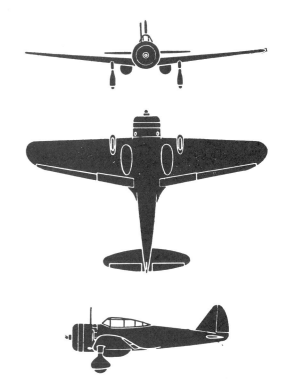

DISTINGUISHING FEATURES: Single radial engine low-wing monoplane. Wings have full dihedral. Both edges tapered with more pronounced taper on the trailing edge. Trailing edge fairs into fuselage. Stubby round nose. Two fuel tank bulges show below wings. Fuselage tapers back to tapered fin with oval rudder. Elliptical stabilizer and elevator. Fixed landing gear with wheel fairings. Rudder ends above fuselage.

INTEREST: This single seat Japanese fighter has a high rate of climb and good maneuverability. Aircraft has nonretractable landing gear. As is the case with "Zeke," fuel tanks are not self-sealing. "Nate" has no armor protection for the pilot. Its armament consists of four 7.7-mm. machine guns. The type 1 SSF "Oscar" is probably a development of "Nate."

SPAN: 35 ft. 10 in.
LENGTH: 24 ft. 4 in.
APPROX. SPEED: 280 m. p. h. at 13,000 ft.

SERVICE CEILING:
33,000 ft.

RESTRICTED

"ZEKE" (ZERO) TYPE 0 MK. 1 F

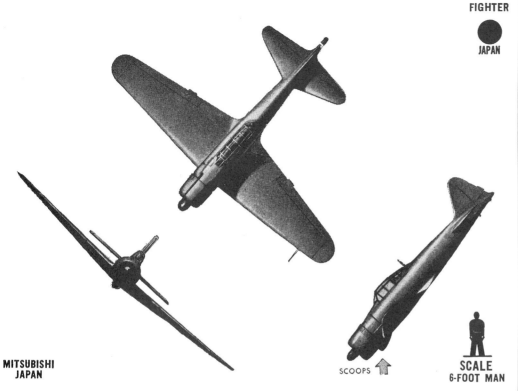

**MITSUBISHI
JAPAN**

SCOOPS

**SCALE
6-FOOT MAN**

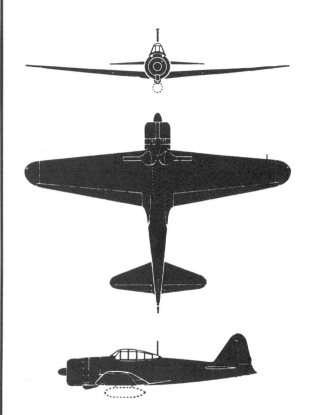

DISTINGUISHING FEATURES: Radial engine, low-wing monoplane. Wings have dihedral from the roots with nearly equal taper and rounded tips. Round nose with medium large spinner. Air scoops for oil cooler and carburetor show below cowling. Fuselage tapers back neatly to a point in rear of tail assembly. Cockpit canopy sits on top of fuselage. Rather large fin and rudder has pronounced taper on leading edge and slight taper on trailing edge.

INTEREST: This famous Japanese fighter, popularly known as the Zero and much respected by U. S. fliers, is the one most frequently shot down. Although "Zeke" is well built, its speed and maneuverability were obtained by light wing loading, largely through the omission of armor. Our fliers quickly found "Zeke's" weakness: no armor protection for pilots or fuel tanks. It has a steep angle of climb, and favors climbing tactics, but above 300 m. p. h., the aircraft is very difficult to roll.

SPAN: 39 ft. 5 in.
LENGTH: 30 ft. 3 in.
APPROX. SPEED: 326 m. p. h. at 16,000 ft.

SERVICE CEILING: 38,500 ft.

APRIL 1943
FROM DATA CURRENTLY AVAILABLE

WAR DEPARTMENT FM 30–30
NAVY DEPARTMENT BUAER 3

RESTRICTED

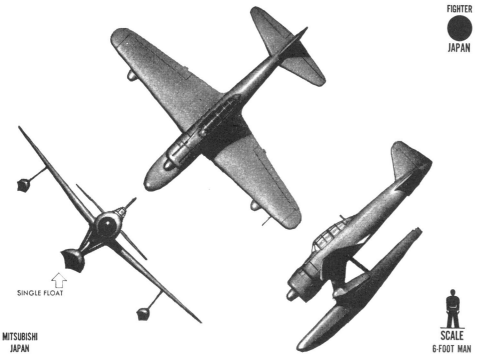

SINGLE FLOAT

MITSUBISHI
JAPAN

SCALE
6-FOOT MAN

DISTINGUISHING FEATURES: Nearly the same as Zeke except for pontoon, wing-tip floats and rounded trailing edge of rudder. Radial engine, low-wing monoplane with single float. Wings have dihedral from the roots with nearly equal taper and rounded tips. Blunt nose with rather large spinner. Carburetor airscoop below cowling. Tapering fuselage. Cockpit canopy placed on top of fuselage. Tapered tailplane with round tips set forward of rudder. Tapered fin and rudder with trailing edge curved into fuselage at the bottom.

INTEREST: The float plane version of the Zero, Rufe is also manufactured by Mitsubishi. The additional drag and weight of the floats are responsible for a decrease in speed of approximately 50 m. p. h. and some loss in maneuverability. This plane was extensively used by the Jap forces in the Aleutians and is in operation in the Southwest Pacific.

NOV. 1943
FROM DATA CURRENTLY AVAILABLE

SUPPLEMENT ONE [WAR DEPARTMENT FM 30—30
NAVY DEPARTMENT BUAER 3

RUFE

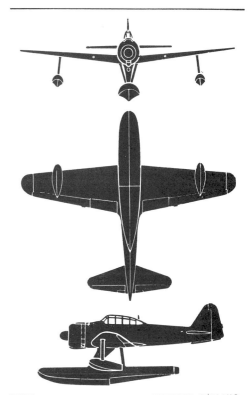

SPAN: 39 ft. 5 in.

LENGTH: 33 ft. 10 in.

APPROX. SPEED: 278 m. p. h. at 16,000 ft.

SERVICE CEILING:
About 35,400 ft.

RESTRICTED

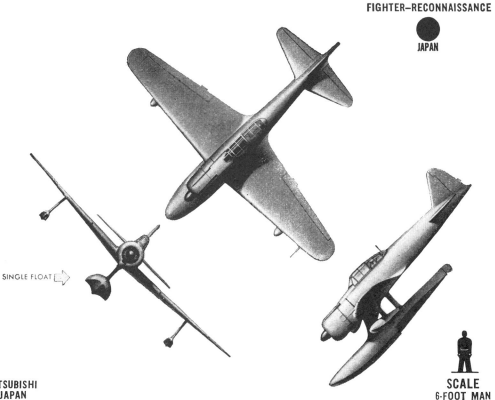

SINGLE FLOAT →

**MITSUBISHI
JAPAN**

SCALE
6-FOOT MAN

DISTINGUISHING FEATURES: Same as Type "O" SSF "Zeke" except for large central pontoon and wing-tip floats. Radial engine low-wing monoplane. Wings have dihedral from the roots with nearly equal taper and rounded tips. Round nose with medium large spinner. Oil cooler scoop and carburetor air scoop show below cowling. Fuselage tapers neatly back to a point in the rear of tail assembly. Cockpit canopy sits on top of fuselage. Rather large fin and rudder with pronounced taper to leading edge and slight taper to trailing edge.

INTEREST: The float plane version of the Zero, "Rufe" is also manufactured by Mitsubishi. The additional drag and weight of the floats are responsible for a decrease in speed of approximately 50 miles an hour. In other respects the float plane approximates the well-known "Zeke," although less maneuverable.

APRIL 1943
FROM DATA CURRENTLY AVAILABLE

WAR DEPARTMENT FM 30–30
NAVY DEPARTMENT BUAER 3

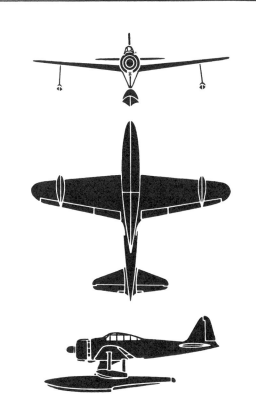

SPAN: 39 ft. 5 in.
LENGTH: 34 ft. 10 in.
APPROX. SPEED: 277 m. p. h. at 15,200 ft.

SERVICE CEILING:
about 36,500 ft.

RESTRICTED

SQUARE TIPS

MITSUBISHI
JAPAN

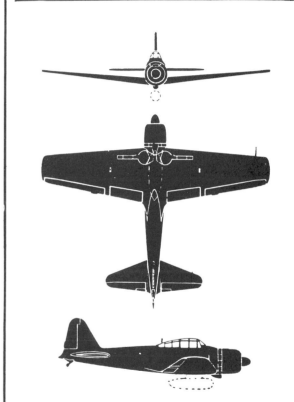

JETTISONABLE
BELLY TANKS

SCALE
6-FOOT MAN

DISTINGUISHING FEATURES: Single radial engine low-wing monoplane. Similar to "Zeke" but with square wing tips and air scoop inside and at top of cowling.
INTEREST: This fighter appears to be more maneuverable than "Zeke." Its rate of climb is estimated to be 2,800 ft. per minute. The aircraft carries two 7.7-mm. machine guns, synchronized to fire through the propeller and two 20-mm. cannon, fixed, are in each wing. "Hap" is apparently a Mark II of "Zeke," with the folding wing tips removed and replaced by a blunt fairing. The position of the air scoop has also been changed, it now being in the top forward edge of the cowling instead of on the outside of the bottom of the cowling. The engine is a Nakajima "Sakae 21" instead of the Nakajima "Sakae 12" in "Zeke," and may develop more horsepower than the "Sakae 12."

SPAN: 36 ft.
LENGTH: 28 ft.
APPROX. SPEED: 338 m. p. h. at 17,200 ft.

SERVICE CEILING: 38,800 ft.

RESTRICTED

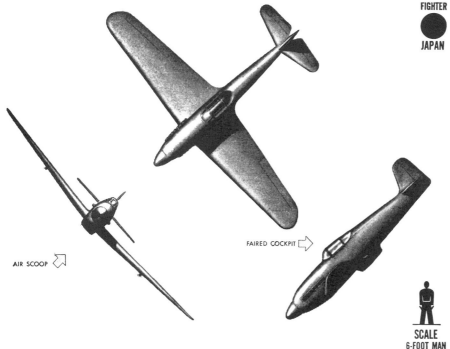

AIR SCOOP �ᐃ

FAIRED COCKPIT ⇨

SCALE
6-FOOT MAN

JAPAN

DISTINGUISHING FEATURES: Single inline engine, low-wing monoplane. Wings have dihedral from roots and moderate taper on both edges. Long nose. Small cockpit faired into the fuselage. Large airscoop extends beyond trailing edge of wing. Bell-shaped fin and rudder. Tailplane has rounded tips, tapered leading edge and **V** cut-out in the elevator.

INTEREST: Fuselage and tail assembly of this single-seat Jap fighter are similar to the He 113. Wings longer and narrower. For the first time, armor plate placed behind the pilot was found in a Jap fighter. Power plant is a 12-cylinder 60° **V**-type liquid-cooled engine. Est. hp. is 1,060 at 15,000 ft. Fuel tanks, in fuselage and wing roots, are leak-proof. Armament: 2 x 12.7 mm. machine guns firing through propeller, 2 x 7.7 mm. machine guns in wings. Provision is made for cannon installation in propeller hub.

NOV. 1943
FROM DATA CURRENTLY AVAILABLE

SUPPLEMENT ONE ⎡ WAR DEPARTMENT FM 30—30
　　　　　　　⎣ NAVY DEPARTMENT BUAER 3

TONY

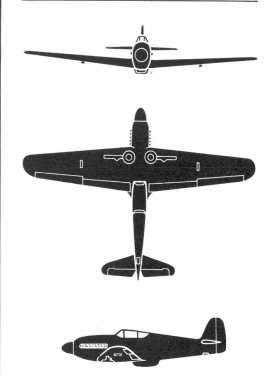

SPAN: 38 ft. 5 in.　　**SERVICE CEILING:**
LENGTH: 30 ft.　　　　　　　35,700 ft.
ESTIMATED SPEED: 363 m. p. h. at 17,000 ft.

RESTRICTED

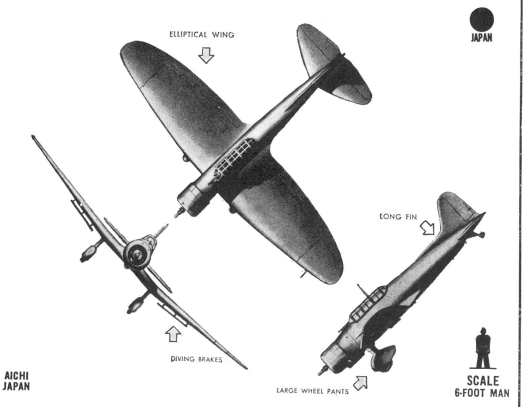

ELLIPTICAL WING

LONG FIN

DIVING BRAKES

AICHI
JAPAN

LARGE WHEEL PANTS

SCALE
6-FOOT MAN

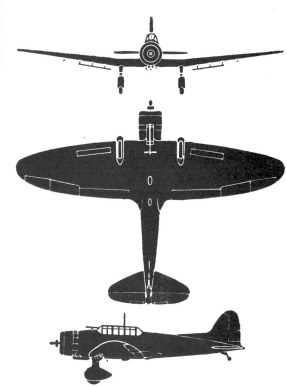

DISTINGUISHING FEATURES: Radial engine low-wing monoplane. Fixed landing gear and junkers dive-brakes. Wings have medium taper and rounded tips. Slim tapering fuselage with protruding cockpit enclosure. Fin faired well forward on fuselage. Sharp taper to leading edge of stabilizer.

INTEREST: These Aichi-made planes were among those which struck so suddenly at Pearl Harbor defenses. It is the standard Jap Navy dive bomber, with two 7.7 mm. machine guns in the top forward cowling and one 7.7 mm. flexible gun in the rear cockpit. It has no armor nor does it have self-sealing gas tanks. Later models may possibly have retractable undercarriages.

SPAN: 47 ft. 7 in.
LENGTH: 32 ft. 10 in.
APPROX. SPEED: 220 m. p. h. at 7,500 ft.

SERVICE CEILING.
27,000 ft.

APRIL 1943
FROM DATA CURRENTLY AVAILABLE

WAR DEPARTMENT FM 30—30
NAVY DEPARTMENT BUAER 3

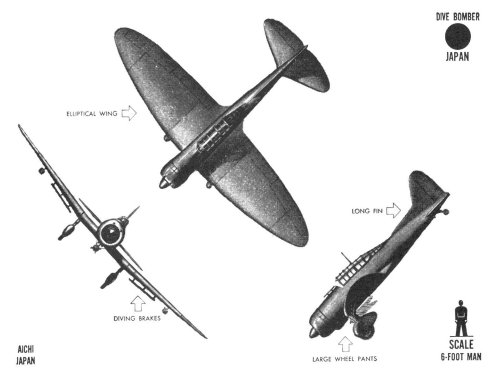

ELLIPTICAL WING ⇨

LONG FIN ⇨

DIVING BRAKES ⇧

LARGE WHEEL PANTS ⇧

**AICHI
JAPAN**

DIVE BOMBER

JAPAN

SCALE
6-FOOT MAN

VAL II

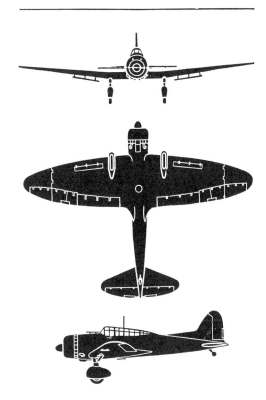

DISTINGUISHING FEATURES: Single radial engine, low-wing monoplane. Wings have marked dihedral outboard of center sections. Elliptical-shaped wings with rounded tips and fillets. Long cockpit enclosure centered above wings fairs smoothly into fuselage. Bell-shaped fin and rudder fairs forward into fuselage. Tailplane has elliptical trailing edge and tapered leading edge. Fixed landing gear with wheel pants.

INTEREST: This second version of Val has a more powerful engine, faired cockpit enclosure, and narrower stabilizer. Armament consists of two 7.7-mm. machine guns in the top forward cowling and one 7.7-mm. flexible gun in the rear cockpit. Normal bomb load is 550 lb. Maximum bomb load is 1,050 lb. Val has been an effective but not a high performance dive bomber. Short dives at a 70° angle can be made. The customary angle is about 55°. No armor or self-sealing tanks have been found.

SPAN: 47 ft. 8 in.
LENGTH: 33 ft. 9 in.
MAX. SPEED: 254 m. p. h. at 13,000 ft.

SERVICE CEILING:
29,800 ft.

RESTRICTED

SWEPT FORWARD

WIDE ROOT AND
TAPERED FILLET

TAILPLANE
TAPERING

WHEELS
EXTEND SLIGHTLY

GREENHOUSE
VERY LONG

SCALE
6-FOOT MAN

NAKAJIMA
(ALSO MFG. BY MITSUBISHI)
JAPAN

DISTINGUISHING FEATURES: Low-wing radial engine monoplane. Outer panels of wings have marked dihedral. Tapered wings with elliptical tips. Round fuselage, blunt nose. A long horizontal cockpit enclosure protrudes above fuselage. Triangular fin and rudder with rounded top.
INTEREST: This navy torpedo bomber, originally manufactured by Nakajima and now also made by Mitsu-

bishi, carries a crew of two, when used as a torpedo bomber, and a crew of three when used on other bombing operations. It lacks self-sealing gas tanks and it has no armor. At a cruising speed of 190 miles per hour, it has a normal range of 495 miles. For armament it has two 7.7 mm. fixed machine guns above the engine cowling, and one 7.7 mm. flexible machine gun in the rear cockpit.

SPAN: 52 ft.
LENGTH: 34 ft.
APPROX. SPEED: 225 m. p. h. at 8,000 ft.

SERVICE CEILING:
27,500 ft

"DAVE" TYPE 95 0-F /P

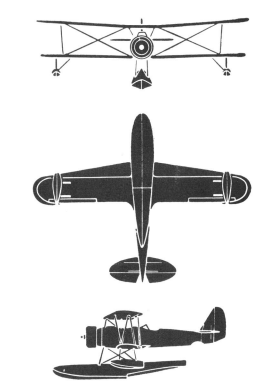

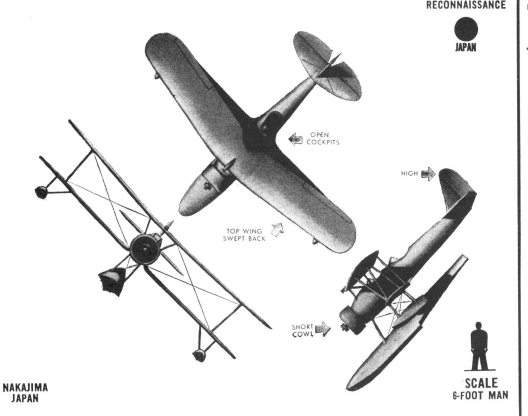

OPEN
COCKPITS

HIGH

TOP WING
SWEPT BACK

SHORT
COWL

SCALE
6-FOOT MAN

**NAKAJIMA
JAPAN**

DISTINGUISHING FEATURES: Single radial engine biplane equipped with single pontoon and fixed wing tip floats. Upper wing swept back, lower wing square to fuselage. Rounded tips. Wings have N-shaped struts. Engine has prominent ring cowling. Fuselage tapers smoothly with two open cockpits. Oval fin and rudder. Elliptical stabilizer and elevator with V cut-out on trailing edge.

INTEREST: Australian reports have indicated that steep dive bombing has been done by this Nakajima product, now manufactured by both Nakajima and Mitsubishi. It carries a crew of two, a bomb load up to 500 lbs., and has two 7.7 mm. machine guns. The forward gun is fixed and the rear gun, firing from the rear cockpit, is flexible. It carries no armor and the fuel tanks lack the self-sealing feature.

SPAN: 36 ft.
LENGTH: 28 ft. 4 in.
APPROX. SPEED: 155 m. p. h. at 12,000 ft.

SERVICE CEILING.
23,000 ft.

RESTRICTED

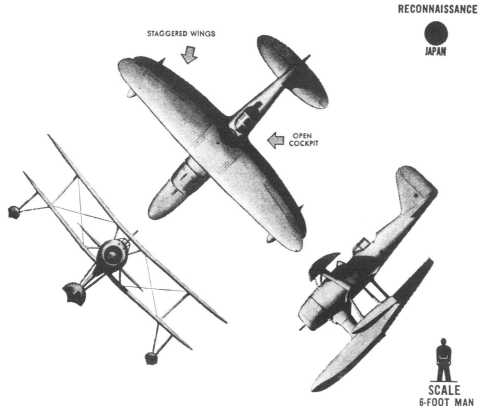

STAGGERED WINGS

OPEN COCKPIT

SASEBO
JAPAN

SCALE
6-FOOT MAN

"PETE" TYPE 0 0-F/P

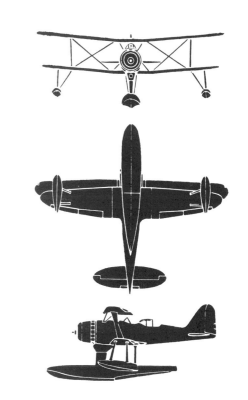

DISTINGUISHING FEATURES: Radial engine biplane equipped with large central pontoon and fixed wing floats. Wings have tapered leading edges, giving a swept back appearance, and large round tips. Fuselage has normal cowling for a radial engine, well streamlined. Tapering fin. Trailing edge of rudder nearly vertical.

APRIL 1943
FROM DATA CURRENTLY AVAILABLE

INTEREST: This two-place float plane of the Japanese Navy is a product of the Sasebo naval arsenal. It may carry a bomb load up to 500 lbs. in two small bomb racks located under the lower wings. For armament, it mounts two 7.7 mm. fixed machine guns, which fire through the propeller and one 7.7 mm. flexible machine gun, operating from the rear cockpit. Self-sealing gas tanks are not a part of "Pete's" equipment.

SPAN: 37 ft.
LENGTH: 34 ft. 6 in.
APPROX. SPEED: 198 m. p. h. at 5,000 ft.

SERVICE CEILING:
29,000 ft.

RESTRICTED

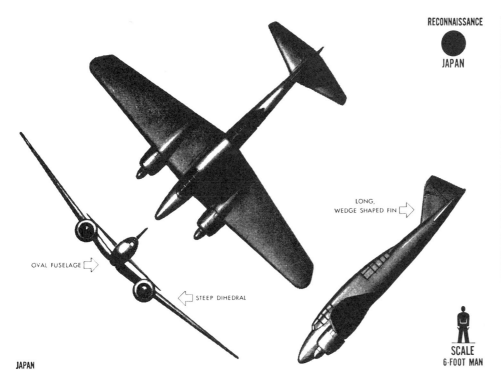

RECONNAISSANCE

JAPAN

LONG,
WEDGE SHAPED FIN →

OVAL FUSELAGE ⇨

← STEEP DIHEDRAL

SCALE
6-FOOT MAN

DINAH

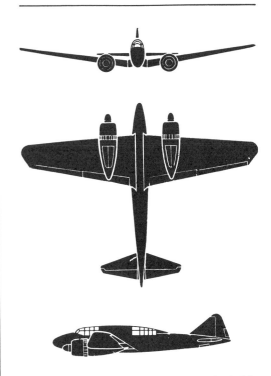

SPAN: 50 ft. (est.)   **SERVICE CEILING:**
LENGTH: 38 ft. (est.)   34,700 ft.
MAX. SPEED: 343 m. p. h. at 13,000 ft.

JAPAN

DISTINGUISHING FEATURES: Twin radial engine, low-wing monoplane. Tapered wing with raked tips. Deep, narrow, oval-shaped fuselage with pointed nose extending beyond nacelles. Long, raised canopy with unglazed center section over wing. Triangular-shaped fin and rudder, wide at base. Tailplane has marked taper on both edges, with small raked tips.

INTEREST: This aircraft is used principally for special reconnaissance missions. Its range is estimated at 1,105 miles at normal cruising speed of 251 m. p. h. The power plant consists of two 14-cylinder air-cooled radial engines developing 1,030 hp. at 10,800 feet.

RESTRICTED

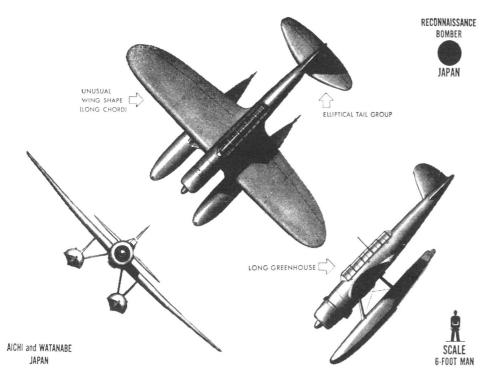

UNUSUAL
WING SHAPE
(LONG CHORD)

ELLIPTICAL TAIL GROUP

LONG GREENHOUSE

AICHI and WATANABE
JAPAN

SCALE
6-FOOT MAN

DISTINGUISHING FEATURES: Single radial engine, low-wing monoplane. Stubby wing with tip curves beginning well inboard. Long unfaired greenhouse. Large floats. High semi-elliptical fin and rudder. Tailplane has curved leading and trailing edges.

INTEREST: This plane when first reported was thought to be type 99 dive bomber "Val" equipped with floats. Recent evidence proves this supposition to have been incorrect. The long wing tip curves give the appearance of an elliptical wing. Recent reports state that Allied shipping has been attacked by this floatplane. Its bomb load is reported to be 4 x 60 kg. (132 lb.) bombs. Armament consists of 1 x 7.7-mm. free gun in the dorsal position.

NOV. 1943
FROM DATA CURRENTLY AVAILABLE

SUPPLEMENT ONE [WAR DEPARTMENT FM 30—30
               [NAVY DEPARTMENT BUAER 3

JAKE

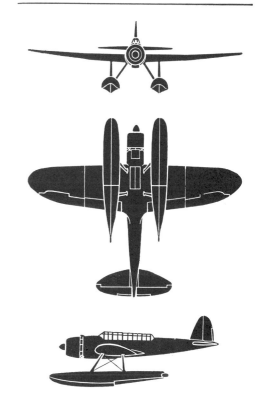

SPAN: 47 ft. 6 in.
LENGTH: 35 ft. 4 in.
MAX. SPEED: 216 m. p. h. at 7,500 ft.

SERVICE CEILING:
24,400 ft.

RESTRICTED

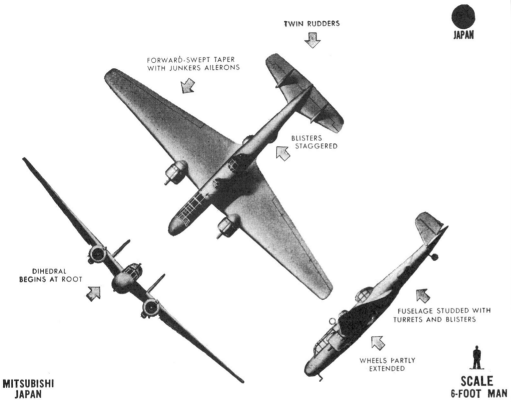

TWIN RUDDERS

FORWARD-SWEPT TAPER
WITH JUNKERS AILERONS

BLISTERS
STAGGERED

DIHEDRAL
BEGINS AT ROOT

FUSELAGE STUDDED WITH
TURRETS AND BLISTERS

WHEELS PARTLY
EXTENDED

**MITSUBISHI
JAPAN**

SCALE
6-FOOT MAN

DISTINGUISHING FEATURES: Two engine mid-wing monoplane. Tapered wings with squared tips. Full-length Junkers type ailerons. Underslung engines. Twin fins and rudders set inboard.

INTEREST: The high level bombing and torpedo attacks made on H. M. S. *Prince of Wales* and H. M. S. *Repulse* were made by these planes. Though the resemblance is rather remote, they are said to have been developed from the Junkers 86 and are used largely for bombing, torpedo dropping, and reconnaissance. Ordinarily the crew was made up of four, but more recently it has been increased to seven. Normal armament is reported to be five 7.7 mm. machine guns. May carry one 20 mm. cannon in dorsal turret.

SPAN: 82 ft.
LENGTH: 54 ft.
APPROX. SPEED: 225 m. p. h. at 7,000 ft.

SERVICE CEILING.
28,000 ft.

"SALLY" TYPE 97 MB

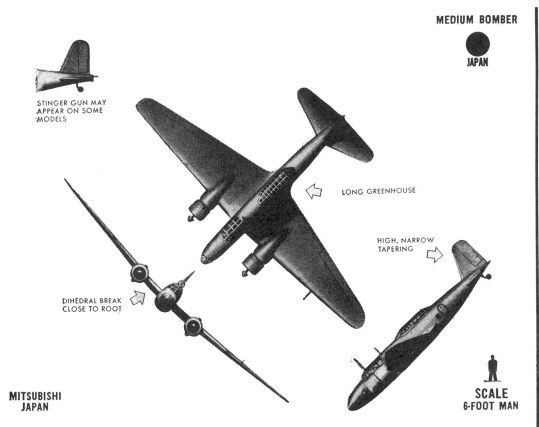

STINGER GUN MAY APPEAR ON SOME MODELS

LONG GREENHOUSE

HIGH, NARROW TAPERING

DIHEDRAL BREAK CLOSE TO ROOT

MITSUBISHI JAPAN

SCALE 6-FOOT MAN

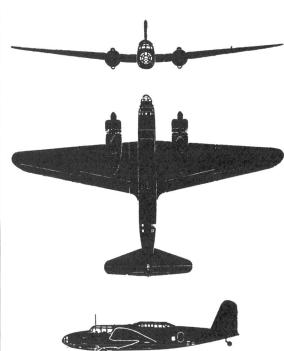

DISTINGUISHING FEATURES: Twin-engine low mid-wing monoplane. Full length dihedral in wings. Trailing edge tapers sharply forward. Elliptical tips. Transparent nose and long dorsal cockpit enclosure, in two sections, extending aft of trailing edge of wing. Single fin and rudder with decided taper on leading edge and vertical trailing edge.

INTEREST: Latest reports indicate little, if any, armor protection for the crew of from five to seven men. Its armament is made up of seven 7.7 mm. flexible machine guns, and sometimes includes a fixed tail gun. In bombing operations the maximum load carried is 4,400 lbs., or normal load of 2,200 lbs. for 670 miles. A development of this aircraft, called "Gwen," and believed to be the "Army Type O twin-engine bomber," has recently been reported.

SPAN: 72 ft.
LENGTH: 47 ft. (approx.)
APPROX. MAX. SPEED: 245 m. p. h. at 8,000 ft.

SERVICE CEILING. about 23,500 ft.

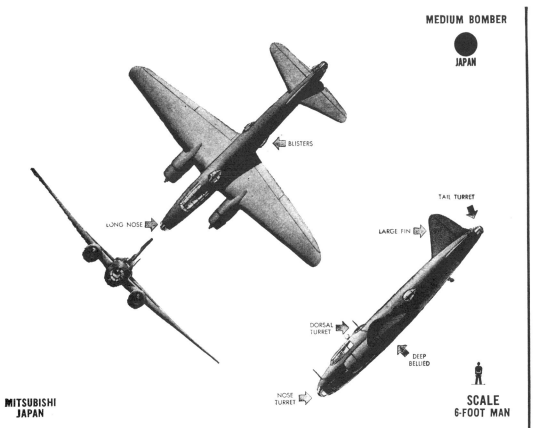

MEDIUM BOMBER

JAPAN

"BETTY" TYPE 1 MB

BLISTERS

LONG NOSE

TAIL TURRET

LARGE FIN

DORSAL
TURRET

DEEP
BELLIED

NOSE
TURRET

SCALE
6-FOOT MAN

**MITSUBISHI
JAPAN**

DISTINGUISHING FEATURES: Twin engine mid-wing monoplane. Dihedral from roots. Wings tapered with rounded tips. Radial engines closely set. Thick fuselage has transparent nose and tail. Dorsal turret and side blisters. Triangular single fin and rudder. Tapered stabilizer.
INTEREST: One of the latest of Japan's bombers, this plane has a high performance and carries a heavy load of bombs or torpedoes. It is in use by both the Japanese Army and Navy and carries a crew of from five to seven. One 7.7 mm. machine gun is mounted in the nose, one in the top turret, and one in each side blister. In addition, it has a 20 mm. cannon in the tail. Although a modified form of self-sealing material has been found on the fuel tanks in the wings, the aircraft is extremely vulnerable to fire.

FROM DATA CURRENTLY AVAILABLE

WAR DEPARTMENT FM 30–30
NAVY DEPARTMENT BUAER 3

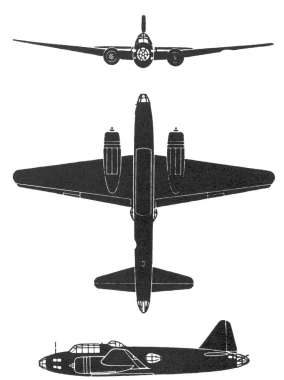

SPAN: 79 ft. 8 in.
LENGTH: 64 ft. (approx.)
APPROX. SPEED: 288 m. p. h. at 13,500 ft.

SERVICE CEILING:
30,000 ft.

RESTRICTED

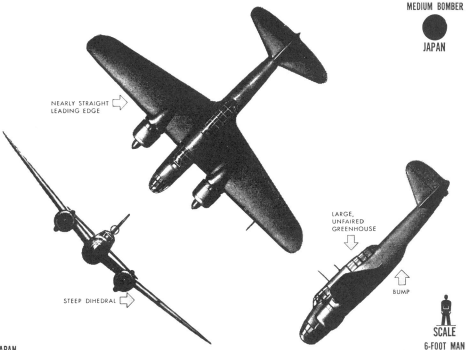

NEARLY STRAIGHT LEADING EDGE

STEEP DIHEDRAL

LARGE, UNFAIRED GREENHOUSE

BUMP

SCALE
6-FOOT MAN

JAPAN

LILY

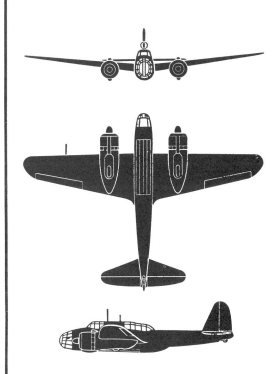

DISTINGUISHING FEATURES: Twin-engine, mid-wing monoplane. Wings are tapered, more on trailing edge than on leading edge. Rounded wing tips. Engines are underslung. Slab-sided fuselage narrows abruptly aft of trailing edge of wing. Rounded nose extends beyond engines and fuselage is broken by large, unfaired greenhouse. Fin and rudder has tapered leading edge with rounded top and curved trailing edge. Tailplane has tapered leading edge, curved trailing edge, with sharply rounded tips.

INTEREST: Lily is often referred to as the "Baltimore" type, since it bears a striking resemblance to the U. S. A–30 Martin "Baltimore" bomber. Carrying a crew of four, Lily is used as a bomber and for reconnaissance. The bomb load carried is 800 pounds stowed internally.

SPAN: 56 ft. 11 in.

LENGTH: 47 ft. 3 in.

SERVICE CEILING:
28,200 ft. with normal load.

ESTIMATED SPEED: 278 m. p. h. at 10,000 ft.

NOV. 1943
FROM DATA CURRENTLY AVAILABLE

SUPPLEMENT ONE [WAR DEPARTMENT FM 30—30
NAVY DEPARTMENT BUAER 3

"MAVIS" TYPE 97 F/B

TAIL TURRET

LONG SPAN

JUNKERS FLAPS

STRUTS

LONG THIN HULL

**KAWANISHI
JAPAN**

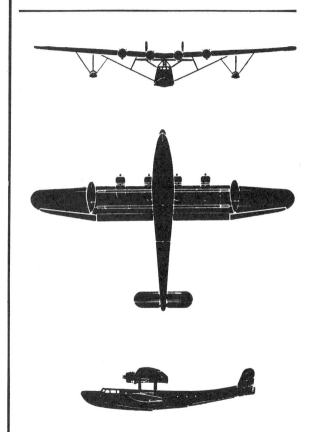

DISTINGUISHING FEATURES: Four-engine parasol monoplane flying boat. Slight dihedral with outer sections tapered. Rounded tips. Engines centered on leading edge; small nacelles. Hull curves up to twin fins and rudders set inboard on stabilizer. Tail turret.

INTEREST: "Mavis" was among the first Japanese aircraft used in bombings over Australia and New Guinea. When carrying their maximum bomb load of 3,300 pounds, they have a range of 2,100 miles, and a crew complement of eight. Armament consists of four 7.7 mm. machine guns; one in the dorsal position, one in the nose, two on the sides, and one 20 mm. cannon in the tail turret.

APRIL 1943
FROM DATA CURRENTLY AVAILABLE

WAR DEPARTMENT FM 30—30
NAVY DEPARTMENT BUAER 3

SPAN: 131 ft.
LENGTH: 82 ft.
APPROX. SPEED: 205 m. p. h. at 8,000 ft.

SERVICE CEILING:
25,000 ft. (normal load)

RESTRICTED

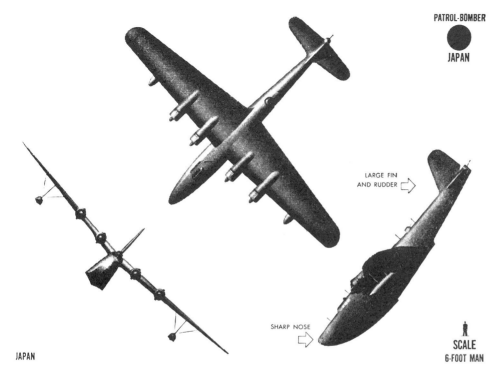

JAPAN

LARGE FIN
AND RUDDER ➪

SHARP NOSE ➪

SCALE
6-FOOT MAN

DISTINGUISHING FEATURES:
Four radial engine, high-wing flying boat. Wing has marked taper from the roots. Trailing edge of wing tip curves sharply to small rounded point. Deep hull has a long nose tapering forward from leading edge of wing. Large high bell-shaped fin and rudder. Tailplane has tapered edges and rounded tips.

INTEREST:
This flying boat is known by the code name of Emily and is one of the largest planes in the Japanese Naval Air Forces. U. S. planes on reconnaissance over Jap-held islands in the Southwest Pacific have reported this plane on several occasions in recent months. Reports indicate that it is operational in limited numbers and that it will be seen more and more frequently.

EMILY

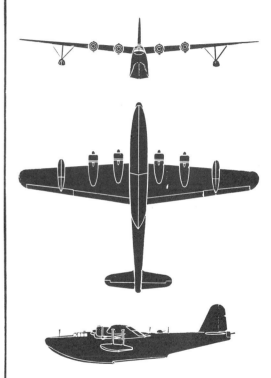

SPAN: 118 ft. (Approx.)　**SERVICE CEILING:**
LENGTH: 90 ft. (Approx.)
MAX. SPEED:

RESTRICTED

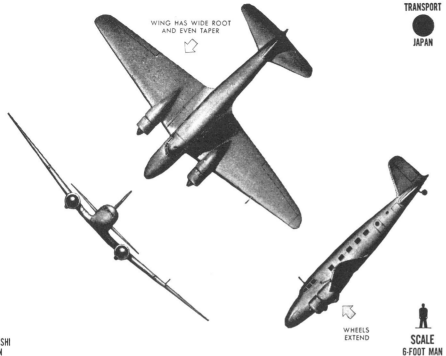

WING HAS WIDE ROOT AND EVEN TAPER

WHEELS EXTEND

SCALE
6-FOOT MAN

MITSUBISHI
JAPAN

TOPSY

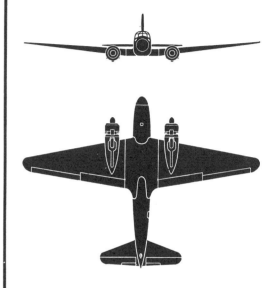

DISTINGUISHING FEATURES: Twin-engine, low-wing monoplane. Wing tapers sharply to rounded tips and has pronounced dihedral. Nose is long and sharply rounded. Fuselage smooth except for break at pilot's cockpit and tapers symmetrically to point at tail. Tail surfaces have pronounced taper on leading edge with rounded tips. Fixed tail wheel, retractable landing gear.

INTEREST: This aircraft has been used in paratroop operations in the Southwest Pacific. It has a cruising range of 1,020 miles with normal fuel and cargo load at an average speed of 197 m. p. h. and at an altitude of 9,200 feet. It is a military version of the Mitsubishi commercial transport, type MC–20, for which sales were solicited in South America before the war.

SPAN: 74 ft.

SERVICE CEILING:
23,000 ft. with normal load

LENGTH: 25 ft. 8 in.

MAX. SPEED: 266 m. p. h. at 10,500 ft.

RESTRICTED

NOV. 1943
FROM DATA CURRENTLY AVAILABLE

SUPPLEMENT ONE [WAR DEPARTMENT FM 30—30
NAVY DEPARTMENT BUAER 3

ITALY: MC-202
   MC-200 (RADIAL ENGINE)
   MC-205 (RADIAL ENGINE)

FIGHTER

ITALY

MACCHI "MC-202"

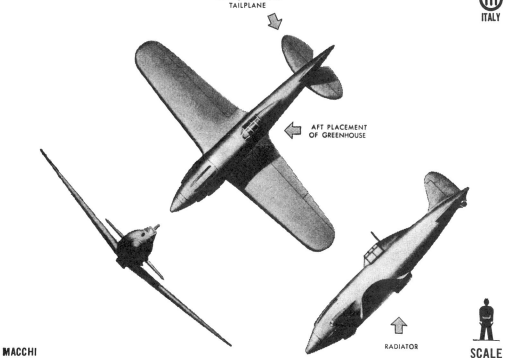

SMALL, ELLIPTICAL TAILPLANE

AFT PLACEMENT OF GREENHOUSE

RADIATOR

MACCHI
ITALY

SCALE
6-FOOT MAN

DISTINGUISHING FEATURES: Single in-line engine, low-wing monoplane. Wings have dihedral from roots with equal taper and rounded tips. Long nose and spinner. Small cockpit canopy. Torpedo-shaped fuselage. Tapered fin and rudder. Elliptical tail plane.

INTEREST: A number of these planes have been used in combat over Egypt, Libya, and Malta. To date, they have had only a little better success than the MC 200,

an earlier version of this plane which has a radial engine. Apparently they are not as fast as they should be, nor are they adequately armed, although they are capable, in some instances, of keeping pace with Allied medium and light bombers. Unlike the MC-200, the cockpit cover of this plane is not transparent all around, and with its lengthened nose, it is questionable whether the pilots of the MC-202 have sufficient visibility.

SPAN: 34 ft. 8 in.
LENGTH: 29 ft. 1 in.
MAX. SPEED: 360 m. p. h. at 20,000 ft.

SERVICE CEILING:
36,000 ft. (max.)

RESTRICTED

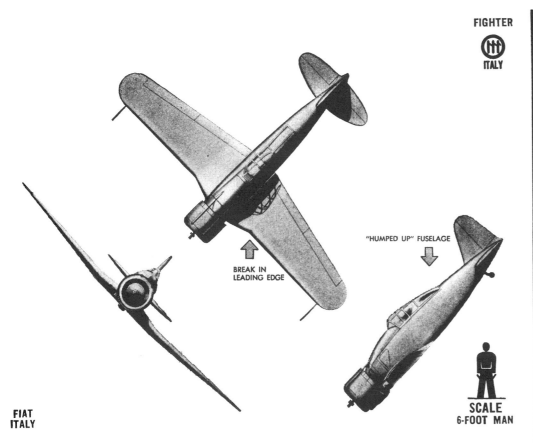

BREAK IN
LEADING EDGE

"HUMPED UP" FUSELAGE

FIGHTER

ITALY

**FIAT
ITALY**

SCALE
6-FOOT MAN

"FIAT G-50"

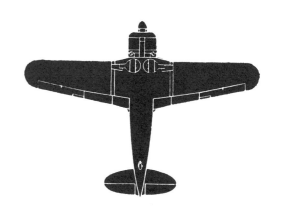

DISTINGUISHING FEATURES: Single radial engine low-wing monoplane. Center section of the wing tapers more sharply than outer sections. Outer sections have moderate taper to rounded tips. Scoop shows below cowling. Narrow fin and rudder with rounded top.

INTEREST: The G-50 has been known as the "Falcon."

It was considered one of the best Italian fighters during the early months after the Battle of France. At the present time its use is much restricted. It has been reported to be difficult to maneuver and unstable. It is of all-metal construction, and the armament consists of two 12.7 mm. machine guns with provision for two 7.7 mm. fixed wing guns.

SPAN: 35 ft. 9 in.
LENGTH: 25 ft. 6 in.
MAX. SPEED: 300 m. p. h. at 14,500 ft.

SERVICE CEILING:
32,500 ft.

APRIL 1943
FROM DATA CURRENTLY AVAILABLE

WAR DEPARTMENT FM 30-30
NAVY DEPARTMENT BUAER 3

ITALY: CANT. Z-1007 bis
Cant. Z-1007 bis (MODIFIED)

MEDIUM BOMBER

ITALY

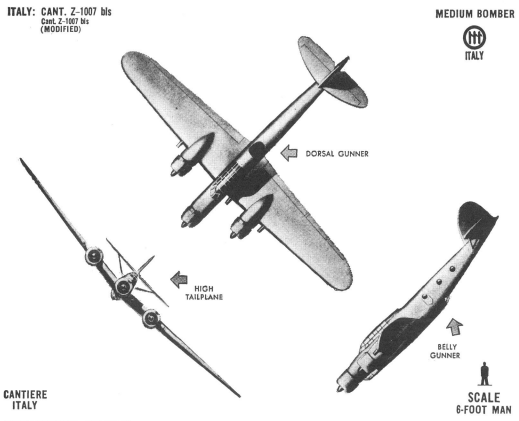

DORSAL GUNNER

HIGH TAILPLANE

BELLY GUNNER

SCALE 6-FOOT MAN

CANTIERE ITALY

DISTINGUISHING FEATURES: Low-wing monoplane with three (3) radial engines. Wings have moderate taper and dihedral. Deep fuselage with raised cabin and bulging bomb aimer's position, bomb bay, and rear ventral gun position. Large curved fin and rudder. Strut braced, elliptical stabilizer and elevator. Later modified version has unbraced twin fins and rudders placed outboard (Photo C).

APRIL 1943
FROM DATA CURRENTLY AVAILABLE

INTEREST: The "Alcione" ("Kingfisher"), as this airplane is called, is one of Italy's best bombers and has been used in every theater of operations in which Italian planes appear. It is constructed of nonstrategic materials such as wood and plywood skin. Its wings are made of plywood, covered with fabric. It will, in all probability, replace the older SM 79. It is believed that it may carry a torpedo stowed internally.

WAR DEPARTMENT FM 30-30
NAVY DEPARTMENT BUAER 3

CANT. "Z-1007"

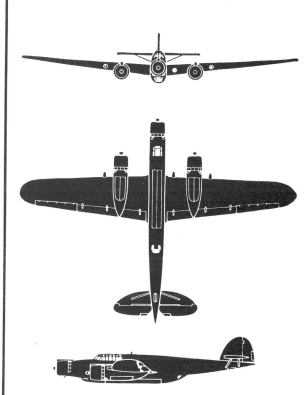

SPAN: 81 ft. 10 in.
LENGTH: 61 ft. 3 in.
MAX. EMERGENCY SPEED: 280 m. p. h. at 15,000 ft.

SERVICE CEILING: 26,500 ft. (normal load)

RESTRICTED

ITALY: Re–2001

Re-2000 (RADIAL ENGINE)
Re-2002 (RADIAL ENGINE)

REGGIANE "RE-2001"

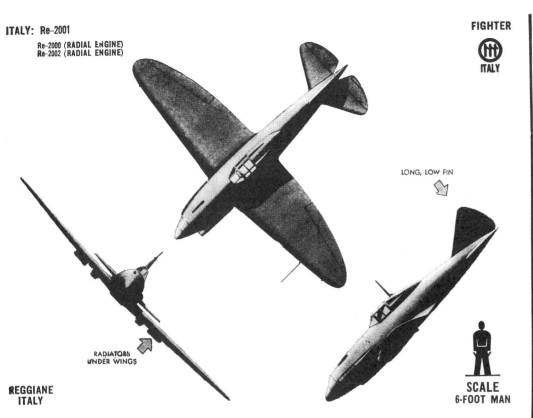

LONG, LOW FIN

RADIATORS UNDER WINGS

REGGIANE ITALY

SCALE
6-FOOT MAN

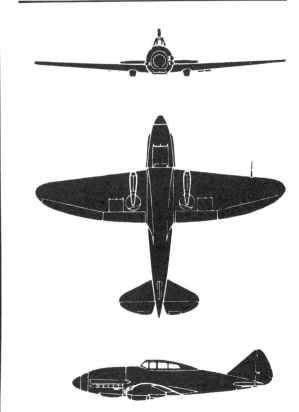

DISTINGUISHING FEATURES: Single in-line engine low-wing monoplane. Wing is elliptical with more curve on trailing edge. Long pointed nose and spinner. Torpedo-shaped fuselage. Prominent cockpit enclosure. Two radiators under wings. Prominent bulging fairings cover landing gear when retracted. Fin tapers backward. Rudder rounded.

INTEREST: Except for its in-line engine, this plane is similar to the Re. 2000 and Re. 2002, which have radial engines. It is one of Italy's best fighters and has frequently been active over Malta. Its armament consists of two synchronized 12.7 mm. guns over the engine and two 7.7 mm. guns in the wings. As with the Re. 2000, the air frame is thought to have been developed from the American Republic Lancer (P-43). Adapted as a fighter bomber, the Re. 2001 may carry an 1,100-lb. bomb under the fuselage. Bomb carriers suitable for dive release may be fitted under the wings. It is nicknamed "Falco II" (the "Falcon II").

SPAN: 36 ft.
LENGTH: 27 ft. 4 in.
MAX. EMERGENCY SPEED: 350 m. p. h. at 20,000 ft.

SERVICE CEILING:
34,000 ft. (normal load)

RESTRICTED

SAVOIA-MARCHETTI "SM-79"

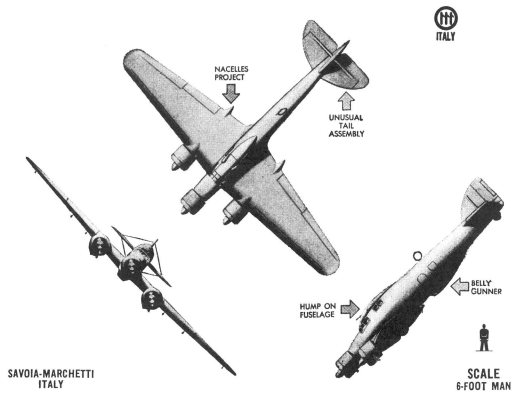

NACELLES PROJECT

UNUSUAL TAIL ASSEMBLY

HUMP ON FUSELAGE

BELLY GUNNER

SCALE
6-FOOT MAN

**SAVOIA-MARCHETTI
ITALY**

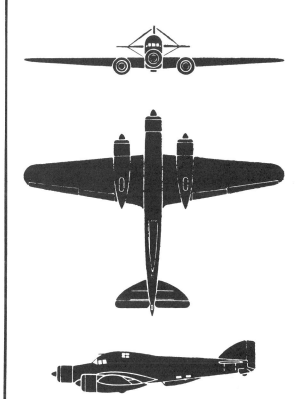

DISTINGUISHING FEATURES: Three-engine, low-wing monoplane. Tapered wings with more pronounced taper on trailing edge. Fuselage is humped at cockpit and tapers backward toward a low fin. Large radial motors. Ventral gondola visible. Rudder has straight trailing edge.

INTEREST: This is Italy's standard long-range bomber and Mussolini has more squadrons of this type than of any other bomber. It has served in Spain, and has been very extensively used in Africa, Albania, and over the Mediterranean. It has been used for torpedo attacks and it is interesting to note that the Allies consider Italian Torpedo Squadrons to be the most efficient in the Italian Air Force. Their torpedoes are believed to be superior to those of the Germans.

SPAN: 69 ft. 6 in.
LENGTH: 54 ft. 6 in.
MAX. EMERGENCY SPEED: 255 m. p. h. at 12,500 ft.
SERVICE CEILING: 23,000 ft. (normal load)

RESTRICTED

ITALY: FIAT BR-20

JAPAN: "RUTH"

MEDIUM BOMBER—TRANSPORT

ITALY   JAPAN

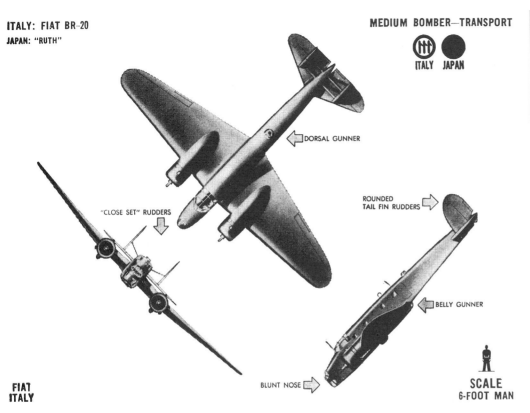

← DORSAL GUNNER

"CLOSE SET" RUDDERS

ROUNDED
TAIL FIN RUDDERS

← BELLY GUNNER

BLUNT NOSE ⇨

**FIAT
ITALY**

**SCALE
6-FOOT MAN**

FIAT "BR-20"

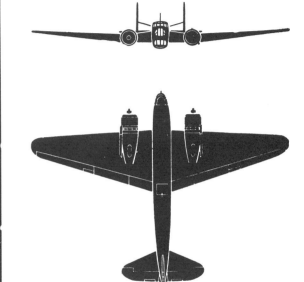

SPAN: 70 ft. 6 in.
LENGTH: 52 ft. 10 in.
MAX. SPEED: 255 m. p. h. at 13,500 ft.

SERVICE CEILING:
25,000 ft. (normal load)

RESTRICTED

DISTINGUISHING FEATURES: Twin radial engine, mid-wing monoplane. Wings have moderate dihedral and extreme taper on trailing edge. Tapered fuselage houses dorsal turret and semiretractable ventral gun mounting. Elliptical strut-braced twin fins and rudders set inboard. Stabilizer and elevator have tapered leading edge and straight trailing edge.

INTEREST: The Br-20 is of all-metal construction. The fuselage aft of the wings is built of welded steel tubing with fabric covering. The forward part of the fuselage is of light metal construction. In November 1940, a flight of these bombers made one disastrous sortie against England from Belgian bases. It was never tried again. Its normal crew is five and it carries a maximum load of 3,500 lbs. of bombs for a range of 1,500 miles. In Italy it is known as the "Cicogna" which means "Stork." The Japanese bought a number of these bombers before the war, some of which have recently been reported in operational use.

APRIL 1943
FROM DATA CURRENTLY AVAILABLE

WAR DEPARTMENT FM 30–30
NAVY DEPARTMENT BUAER 3

YAK-1 (I-26)

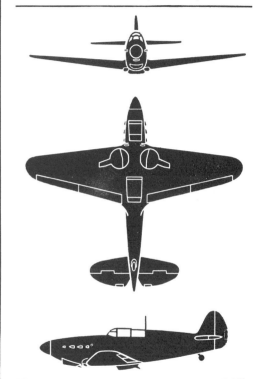

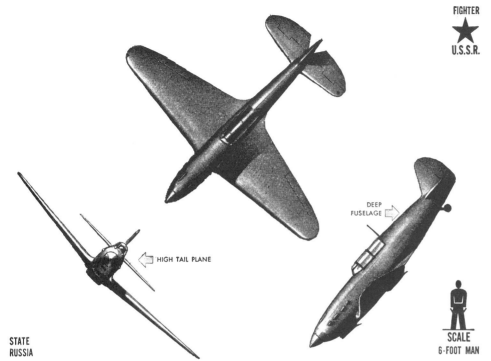

HIGH TAIL PLANE

DEEP FUSELAGE

STATE
RUSSIA

SCALE
6-FOOT MAN

DISTINGUISHING FEATURES: Single inline engine, low-wing monoplane. Wings have nearly equal taper with large fillets. Long pointed nose with large spinner. Oil cooler shows under the nose. Radiator is placed well aft. Cockpit is centered amidships. Fin tapers forward with rounded top. Rudder is rounded. Tailplane has elliptical trailing edge and large V cut-out.

INTEREST: This airplane was designed by Alexander Yakovlev, who was also responsible for the Yak–4. It has been reported in action on the northwestern front. The rear fuselage appears to have a fabric covering. The landing gear retracts inward and is well covered by fairing plates. The appearance of the exhausts indicates that the engine is of the Hispano-Suiza type.

SPAN: 32 ft. 10 in.
LENGTH: 27 ft. 11 in.
MAX. SPEED: 315 m. p. h. at 14,000 ft.

SERVICE CEILING: 30,500 ft.

RESTRICTED

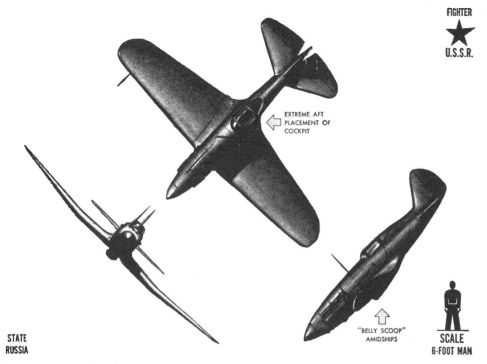

FIGHTER

★

U.S.S.R.

EXTREME AFT
PLACEMENT OF
COCKPIT

"BELLY SCOOP"
AMIDSHIPS

SCALE
6-FOOT MAN

STATE
RUSSIA

MIG-3 (I-18)

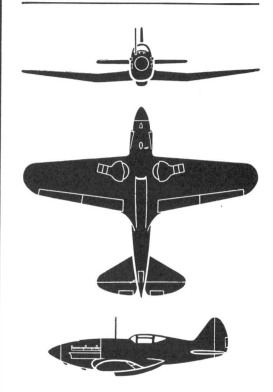

DISTINGUISHING FEATURES: Single inline engine, low-wing monoplane. Slight inverted gull wing with rounded tips. Leading edge has slight taper; trailing edge sharp taper. Trailing edges faired into fuselage. Long nose with large pointed spinner. Small cockpit set over trailing edge of wing. Fin and stabilizer taper well forward. Rounded trailing edge on rudder and elevators. V cut-out in center of elevators.

INTEREST: A modern liquid-cooled fighter, the Mig-3 was constructed after the start of the war and was developed largely from the I-16 ("Mosca") which had seen combat service in the Spanish Revolution. As in other Russian planes, the I-18 makes noticeable use of intermixed wood and metal construction. It is one of Russia's best fighters and has met with outstanding success in encounters with the best planes of the Luftwaffe. This fighter played a large part in holding the Germans before Moscow in 1941.

SPAN: 34 ft. 6 in.
LENGTH: 26 ft. 8 in.
APPROX. SPEED: 375 m. p. h. at 22,000 ft.

SERVICE CEILING:
34,000 ft.

RESTRICTED

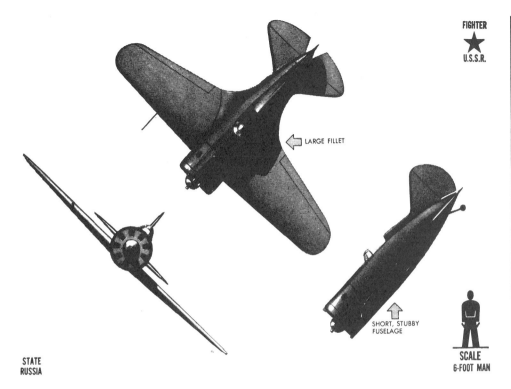

LARGE FILLET

SHORT, STUBBY FUSELAGE

STATE
RUSSIA

SCALE
6-FOOT MAN

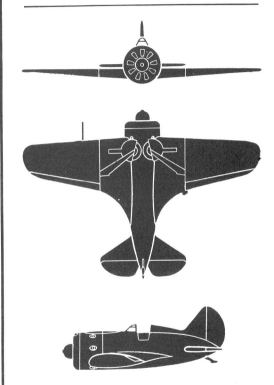

I-16; I-16C

DISTINGUISHING FEATURES: Single radial engine, low-wing monoplane. Wing has straight leading edge, tapered trailing edge and rounded tips. Very large wing fillets extend well back toward tail. Fuselage very short and stubby with large cylindrical nose. Small cockpit set well back with head fairing extending to fin. Rudder has round trailing edge. Stabilizer has leading edge tapered forward. Elevators have cut-out in center.

INTEREST: This monoplane received thorough testing in the Spanish Civil War. It has been handicapped in maneuverability due to high wing loading. As used in Spain, the I–16 had armor plate or 7 mm. thickness, which protected the back and head of the pilot. This plane, although obsolete, is used as a fighter and advanced trainer. The current model, the I–16C or "Super Rata," has a 1,000 hp. engine. The older I–16 is sometimes called the "Rata" or "Mosca."

SPAN: 29 ft. 2 in.
LENGTH: 20 ft. 4 in.
APPROX. SPEED: 300 m. p. h. at 15.000 ft.

SERVICE CEILING:
32,000 ft.

RESTRICTED

NOV. 1943
FROM DATA CURRENTLY AVAILABLE

SUPPLEMENT ONE [WAR DEPARTMENT FM 30—30
NAVY DEPARTMENT BUAER 3

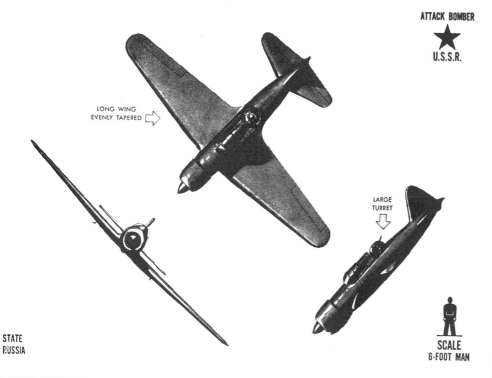

LONG WING
EVENLY TAPERED ⇨

LARGE
TURRET
⇩

STATE
RUSSIA

SCALE
6-FOOT MAN

SU-2

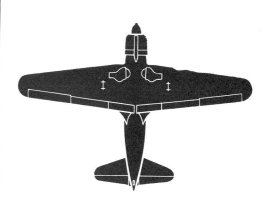

DISTINGUISHING FEATURES: Single radial engine low-wing monoplane. Wings have very little dihedral, equal taper, and rounded tips. Large round nose with prominent spinner. Fuselage has a long transparent canopy with a turret at the rear. Tapered tail surfaces with rounded tips.

INTEREST: The SU–2 is a two-seater general purpose monoplane. Its general appearance is similar to the Brewster Bermuda and Curtiss Helldiver. German sources state that this plane can be used as a four-gun single-seater. The single gun turret is similar to that used on the DB–3 and has an ingenious hinged cupola, half of which opens as an exit.

SPAN: 47 ft. 2 in.
LENGTH: 31 ft. 10 in.
MAX. SPEED: 300 m. p. h. at 21,000 ft.

SERVICE CEILING: 33,000 ft.

RESTRICTED

NOV. 1943
FROM DATA CURRENTLY AVAILABLE

SUPPLEMENT ONE [WAR DEPARTMENT FM 30—30
NAVY DEPARTMENT BUAER 3

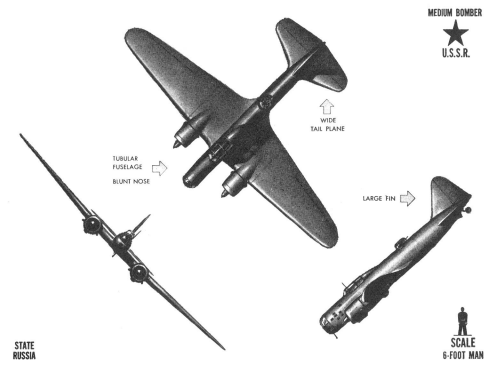

WIDE
TAIL PLANE

TUBULAR
FUSELAGE

BLUNT NOSE

LARGE FIN

STATE
RUSSIA

SCALE
6-FOOT MAN

DB-3

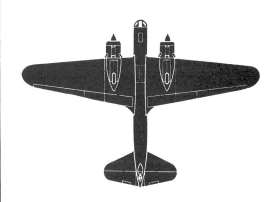

DISTINGUISHING FEATURES: Twin radial engine, low-wing monoplane. Wings have equal taper with rounded tips. Round protruding nose. Top turret is centered between cabin canopy and fin. Large wing root fillets. Triangular fin and rudder with rounded top. Tailplane has more taper on leading edge and rounded tips.

INTEREST: The DB–3 is an all-metal monoplane of sound light-alloy stressed-skin construction. The fuselage is straight with slight taper near the tail. The tail unit has fabric-covered control surfaces. The shape of the tail closely resembles that of the Stormovik. Both airplanes were designed by Serge Ilyushin. This plane is identical in appearance to the DB–3F, except for the nose of the fuselage and the engine cowlings.

SPAN: 70 ft. 2 in.   **SERVICE CEILING:**
LENGTH: 46 ft. 10 in.   25,500 ft.
MAX. SPEED: 260 m. p. h. at 16,000 ft.

NOV. 1943
FROM DATA CURRENTLY AVAILABLE

SUPPLEMENT ONE ⎡ WAR DEPARTMENT FM 30—30
                ⎣ NAVY DEPARTMENT BUAER 3

RESTRICTED

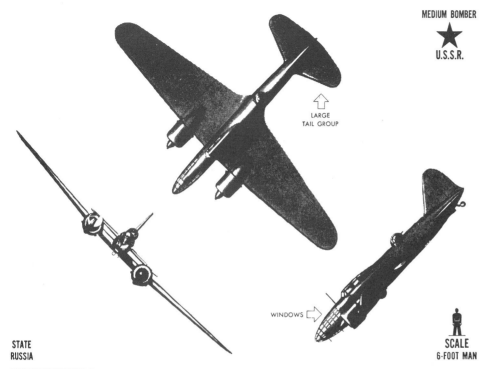

MEDIUM BOMBER

★

U.S.S.R.

LARGE
TAIL GROUP

WINDOWS ⇨

SCALE
6-FOOT MAN

STATE
RUSSIA

DB-3F

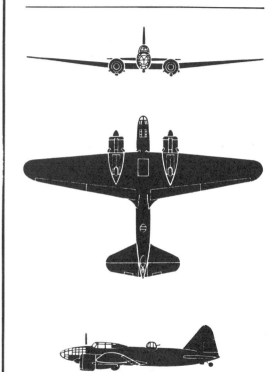

SPAN: 70 ft. 2 in. **SERVICE CEILING:**
LENGTH: 47 ft. 7 in.   29,000 ft.
APPROX. SPEED: 295 m. p. h. at 21,000 ft.

RESTRICTED

DISTINGUISHING FEATURES: Twin radial engine, low-wing monoplane. Trailing edge has pronounced taper and fairs into fuselage. Transparent nose. Raised cockpit canopy. Round turret centered between fin and cockpit. Fin tapers forward. Tapered tailplane with rounded tips.

INTEREST: The DB–3 and DB–3F were developed from the ZKB–26 which flew from Moscow to Miscow Island, New Brunswick, in April 1939. The DB–3F has a streamlined pointed nose instead of a turret and slightly different engine cowlings; otherwise it is identical to the DB–3. The large wing root fillets are characteristic of most Russian types. The M–88 radial engines give about 1,100 hp. and are fitted with two-speed superchargers. Other equipment consists of variable pitch propellers and five 7.6-mm. machine guns. The DB–3F is slightly faster than the DB–3 and when fitted with extra gas tanks it can be used for long range photographic reconnaissance.

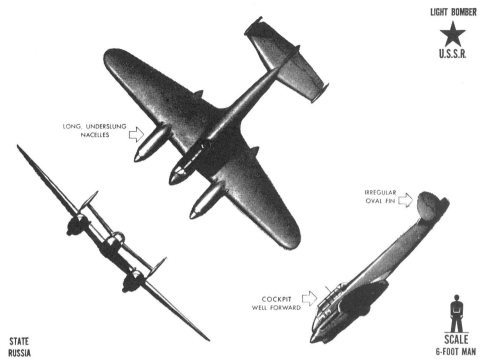

LONG, UNDERSLUNG NACELLES

IRREGULAR OVAL FIN

COCKPIT WELL FORWARD

SCALE
6-FOOT MAN

STATE
RUSSIA

DISTINGUISHING FEATURES: Twin inline engine, low-wing monoplane. Slight taper to leading edge of wing. Trailing edge highly tapered, fairs into fuselage. Engine nacelles protrude beyond trailing edge of wing and beyond nose of fuselage. Protruding cockpit canopy well forward. Twin outboard fin and rudders have distorted circular shape.

INTEREST: One of the Russian high-speed bombers, the Yak–4 has contributed much to the work of the Red Air Force. The construction of the plane is of mixed wood and metal. It carries a crew of two in a well-glazed cockpit. The armament is said to consist of two 20-mm. and four 7.6-mm. machine guns, in addition to a 2,200-lb. bomb load. A semi-retractable ski landing gear may be installed when necessary.

YAK-4

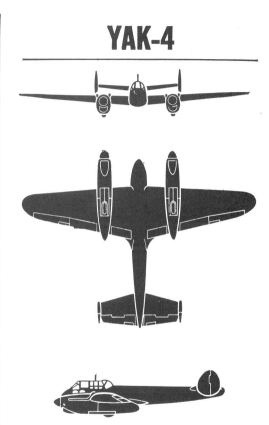

SPAN: 45 ft. 11 in.
LENGTH: 32 ft. 10 in.
MAX. SPEED: 320 m. p. h. at 14,000 ft.

SERVICE CEILING: 27,500 ft.

RESTRICTED

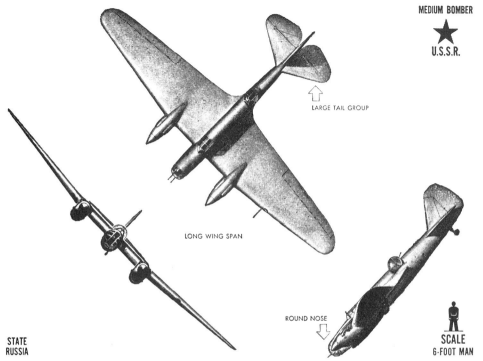

LARGE TAIL GROUP

LONG WING SPAN

ROUND NOSE

MEDIUM BOMBER

U.S.S.R.

SCALE
6-FOOT MAN

STATE
RUSSIA

DISTINGUISHING FEATURES:

Twin-engine, high mid-wing monoplane. Long wing has equally tapered outboard sections with straight leading edge on center section. Liquid-cooled engines have pointed spinners and underslung radiators. Fuselage has rounded nose. Rudder is rounded. Fin tapers forward. Large cut-out in rounded trailing edge of elevators.

INTEREST:

The SB-3 is a three-seater bomber and a later version of the SB-2. It has more powerful engines than the earlier version. Two different styles of cowlings are used to house this engine: One with a ducted underslung radiator and the other with both radiators and oil coolers in the wing. Many SB-3 bombers have dive brakes under the wing, outboard of the nacelles. This bomber is protected by leakproof tanks and armor plate and carries 4 x 7.6-mm. guns. The later models of this plane are equipped with a dorsal turret, whereas the earlier planes had an open gun position with sliding cover identical with that used on the SB-2.

NOV. 1943
FROM DATA CURRENTLY AVAILABLE

SB-3

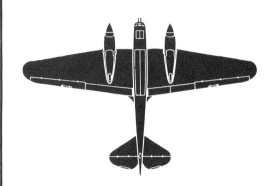

SPAN: 66 ft. 11 in.
LENGTH: 41 ft.
APPROX. SPEED: 260 m. p. h. at 14,000 ft.

SERVICE CEILING:
28,000 ft.

RESTRICTED

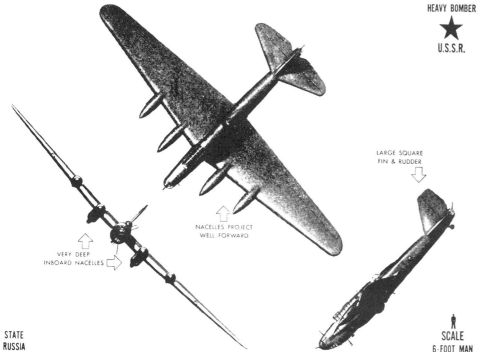

LARGE SQUARE
FIN & RUDDER

NACELLES PROJECT
WELL FORWARD

VERY DEEP
INBOARD NACELLES

SCALE
6-FOOT MAN

STATE
RUSSIA

DISTINGUISHING FEATURES: Four inline engine, mid-wing monoplane. Wings are tapered on both edges with rounded tips. Outboard nacelles small and round. Inboard nacelles very deep with large radiator under engine and gun position in the rear. Raised greenhouse with rear portion covered. Top gun turret. Tailplane is tapered with round tips, while the single fin and rudder is tall and angular.

INTEREST: This is the best known Russian long-range bomber. These planes have raided Berlin, Danzig, and Balkan cities. It is now in large-scale production and is in service with the new bomber command of the Red Air Force. The TB–6B, from which the TB–7 was redesigned, was used in Polar expeditions before the war. The TB–7 carries a crew of about 9 men. Gun positions in the large underslung inboard nacelles are an interesting feature of this aircraft.

TB-7

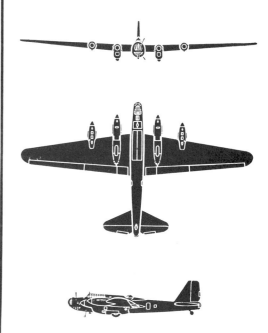

SPAN: 131 ft. 2 in.
LENGTH: 73 ft. 10 in.
MAX. SPEED: 275 m. p. h. at 22,000 ft.

SERVICE CEILING:
36,000 ft.

IL-3; IL-2

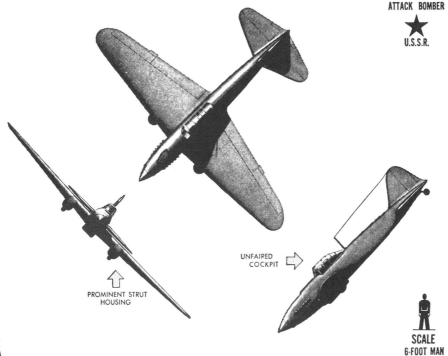

PROMINENT STRUT HOUSING

UNFAIRED COCKPIT ⟹

SCALE
6-FOOT MAN

STATE
RUSSIA

DISTINGUISHING FEATURES: Single inline engine, low-wing monoplane. Wing has pronounced taper and trailing edge fairs into fuselage. Prominent fairings for retractable landing gear beneath wings. Fuselage has rather long nose with pointed spinner and radiator beneath wing. Prominent, unfaired cockpit canopy. Fin and rudder have rounded top. Diamond-shaped tailplane with round tips.

INTEREST: The Stormovik is said to be so heavily armored for strafing work that light cannon fire has small effect on its sides. It is in its element when flying low, attacking German tank and mechanized columns. The engine cowling is composed of steel plate 6- to 8-mm. in thickness, Even parts of the plane which are the least vulnerable have protecting armor of 4 mm. thickness. With heavy armament consisting of two 20- or 37-mm. cannon, plus machine guns, the plane is designed especially to be a "flying anti-tank battery."

SPAN: 47 ft. 11 in.
LENGTH: 38 ft.
MAX. SPEED: 275 m. p. h. at 8,000 ft.

SERVICE CEILING:
28,000 ft.

RESTRICTED

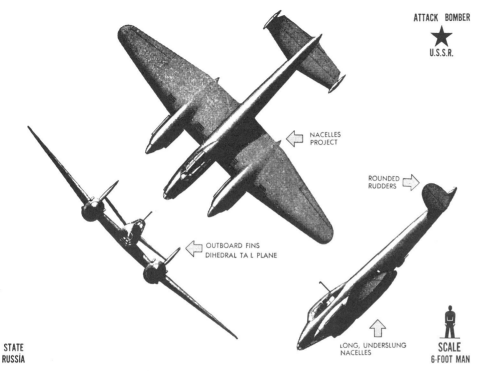

ATTACK BOMBER

★

U.S.S.R.

NACELLES PROJECT ⇐

ROUNDED RUDDERS ⇒

⇐ OUTBOARD FINS DIHEDRAL TA L PLANE

LONG, UNDERSLUNG NACELLES ⇧

SCALE
6-FOOT MAN

**STATE
RUSSIA**

DISTINGUISHING FEATURES: Twin inline engine, low-wing monoplane. Wing has rectangular center·section. Leading edge and trailing edge of outer section equally tapered. Curved tips. Engine nacelles are underslung and project beyond trailing edge. Fuselage has graceful slender taper. Small raised cockpit canopy. Warped oval-shaped fins and rudders mounted outboard on stabilizer which has pronounced dihedral.

INTEREST: The 16th German Army at Starya will remember this plane, which was used to bomb their airfields. The PE–2, a light bomber, has often met German fighters in hand-to-hand combat. Originally designed as a dive bomber, this fast "twin-tail" has performed many kinds of offensive and defensive actions. The fighter version of this plane has no bombardier's windows under the nose and is known as the PE–2B or PE–3.

NOV. 1943
FROM DATA CURRENTLY AVAILABLE

SUPPLEMENT ONE ⌈ WAR DEPARTMENT FM 30—30
NAVY DEPARTMENT BUAER 3

PE-2; PE-2B

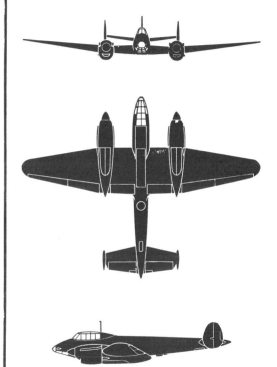

SPAN: 56 ft. 1 in.
LENGTH: 41 ft. 5 in.
APPROX. SPEED: over 300 m. p. h.

SERVICE CEILING:
32,000 ft.

RESTRICTED

RUSSIA: SB-2
GERMANY: B-71

MEDIUM BOMBER
GLIDER TUG

★ ✠
U.S.S.R. REICH

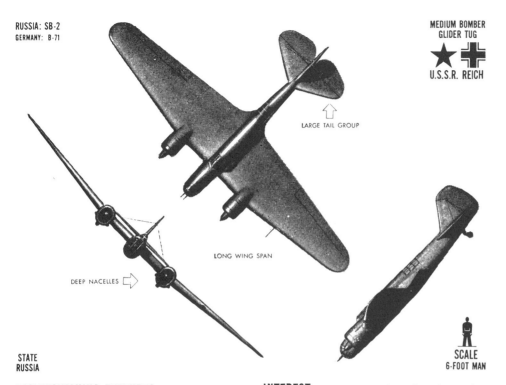

LARGE TAIL GROUP ⬆

LONG WING SPAN

DEEP NACELLES ⬅

STATE
RUSSIA

SCALE
6-FOOT MAN

SB-2

DISTINGUISHING FEATURES: Twin-engine, mid-wing monoplane. Oval-shaped engines. Leading edge of unusually long wing has straight center section and tapered outer sections. Trailing edge tapered with large fillets at fuselage. Round tips. Fuselage has rounded nose. Large fin tapers forward. Rounded rudder. Tailplane has rounded elevators with V cut-out. Leading edge of tailplane tapers forward.

INTEREST: A Soviet bomber of moderate size used in the Spanish Civil War and the Russo-Finnish campaign. Front twin-gun turret has slots for elevation and a limited traverse. Early models had a dorsal gun cockpit with sliding cover. Later models fitted with turret. Semi-retractable ventral gun position aft of rear cockpit. Engines are 860 hp. liquid-cooled V type with automobile-style radiators. Some of these planes, produced in Czechoslovakia, were seized by the Germans and used as glider tugs. German designation is B–71.

SPAN: 66 ft. 11 in.
LENGTH: 41 ft.
MAX. SPEED: 250 m. p. h. at 15,000 ft.

SERVICE CEILING:
27,000 ft.

RESTRICTED

NOV. 1943
FROM DATA CURRENTLY AVAILABLE

SUPPLEMENT ONE [WAR DEPARTMENT FM 30—30
[NAVY DEPARTMENT BUAER 3

AIRCRAFT MANUAL SERIES

Curtiss Standard JN4-D—Jenny
Ford Trimotor
Lockheed P-38 Lightning
Bell P-39 Airacobra
Curtiss P-40 Warhawk
Republic P-47 Thunderbolt
North American F-51 Mustang
Northrop P-61 Black Widow
Chance Vought F4U Corsair
Flying Wings of Northrop
Messerschmitt ME-262 Sturmvogel
DeHavilland Mosquito
Supermarine Spitfire
Hawker Hurricane
Boeing B-17 Flying Fortress
Bell P-63 Kingcobra
X-15 Research Airplane
F-82 Twin Mustang
J-3 Piper Cub
Story of the Texan AT-6
Lockhead F-80 Shooting Star
Grumman F6F Hellcat
B-24 Liberator
Guide to Pre-1930 Aircraft Engines
North American B-25 Mitchell Bomber
Grumman Wildcat
Curtiss OX-5 Aeronautical Engine

TECHNICAL & REFERENCE MANUALS

Helicopter Design and Data Manual
Aircraft Detail Design Manual 2nd Ed.
Aircraft Hardware Standards Manual
 and Engineering Reference
Handbook of Airfoil Sections for Light Aircraft
1929 Airline Schedule of Commercial Transport
World War II International Aircraft
 Recognition Manual

AVIATION PUBLICATIONS

217 E. WASHINGTON ST.
P.O. BOX 357
APPLETON
WISCONSIN 54912
U.S.A.

Litho in U.S.A. at Graphic Communications Center
with production by Badger Printing Division
Appleton, Wisconsin 54912